The Ultimate Cookbook for Young Chef

100+ Easy and Flavorful Baking and Sweet Recipes for

Kids to Cook with Great Funny (Color Edition)

Dale Herbert

Table of Content

Introduction ·· 1

Chapter 1: Welcome to Culinary School ·························· 2

Inside a Chef's Kitchen ······················· 2   Oils ·· 8

How To Become a Good Chef? ············ 6   Serving tips ····························· 10

All About the Ingredients ····················· 7   Setting Up the table ················· 10

Chapter 2: Cakes & Cupcakes ··································· **13**

Angel Food Cake ····························· 13   Dark Chocolate Fudge Lava Cakes ········· 18

Banana Coffee Cake ·························· 13   Dreamy Cheesecake ··················· 19

Chocolate Layer Cake ························ 14   Mini Almond Flourless Chocolate Cakes ········ 19

Epic Pound Cake ······························ 14   Grasshopper Cake Stacks ············· 20

Cinnamon Nut Coffee Cake ················· 15   Rich Chocolate Cupcakes ············· 20

Crumb Cake ···································· 15   Lemon Loaf Cake ······················ 21

Gingerbread Cupcakes ······················ 16   Orange Vanilla Pound Cake ··········· 21

Coconut Explosion Cupcakes ··············· 16   New York–Style Cheesecake ········· 22

Golden Butter Cupcakes ····················· 17   Pick-Your-Flavour Ice Cream Cake ··· 22

Cupcakes With Chocolate Fudge Frosting ······· 17   Upside-Down Apple Cupcakes ········ 23

Chocolate Fudge Layer Cake with Peanut Butter   Zebra Marble Cake with Vanilla Frosting ········ 23

Frosting ··· 18   Sprinkle Cake Pops ···················· 24

Chapter 3: Bread & Muffins ····································· **26**

Chocolate-Glazed Banana Bread Minis ········· 26   Spiced Plum & Quinoa Muffins ·················· 30

Cranberry-Date-Nut Bread ···················· 26   S'mores Muffins ····························· 30

Honey Oat Bread ······························· 27   Yogurt Banana Bread ······················ 31

Lemon-Glazed Earl Grey Tea Bread ············ 27   Corn Muffins ································· 31

Mini Triple Chocolate Muffins ················ 28   Tender Chocolate Chip Mini Muffins ·········· 32

Quick Garlic Bread ···························· 28   Whole-Wheat Raspberry Muffins ··········· 32

Old-Fashioned White Sandwich Bread ········· 29   Basic Muffins ······························· 33

PB&J Muffins··································· 29

Chapter 4: Cookies & Bars ···· 35

Chocolate Pecan Tassie Cookie Cups ········· 35
Crispy Meringue Cookies ········· 35
Classic Lemon Bars ········· 36
Crispy Chocolate Chip Cookies ········· 36
Double Chocolate Chip Cookies ········· 37
Frosted Sugar Cookie Pops ········· 37
Honey Roasted Peanut Butter Cookies ········· 38
Marble Cookies ········· 38
Mini "Black & White" Cookies ········· 39
Oat Pear Bars ········· 39
Pb&J Bars ········· 40
Raspberry-Rhubarb Crumb Bars ········· 40
Rosemary Shortbread Cookies ········· 41
Spiced Oatmeal Raisin Cookies ········· 41
Swap-It-Your-Way Sweet & Salty Cookies ········· 42
Thick And Chewy Chocolate Chip Cookies ········· 42
Strawberry Cheesecake Bars ········· 43

Chapter 5: Pizza ···· 45

Breakfast Pizza ········· 45
Classic Margherita Pizza ········· 45
Mini Mexican Pizzas ········· 46
Personal Margherita Pizzas ········· 46
Pizza Primavera ········· 47
Pizza-Tastic Dough ········· 47
Spicy Sausage & Cheese Pizza ········· 47
Spinach-Artichoke Pizza ········· 48
Thin-Crust Veggie Pizza ········· 48

Chapter 6: Fruit Desserts ···· 50

Banana-Berry Split ········· 50
Flognarde (Apple-Custard Bake) ········· 50
Cheesecake-Stuffed Strawberries ········· 51
Homemade Apple Crisp ········· 51
Lemon Soufflés ········· 52
Peach-Blueberry Crisp ········· 53
Roasted Strawberry Parfait ········· 53
Sautéed Apples ········· 54
Strawberry Granita ········· 54
Watermelon-Lime Sorbet ········· 55
Apple Stuffing ········· 55

Chapter 7: Salad ···· 57

Asian Noodle Salad ········· 57
Chicken Salad Wraps ········· 57
Colourful Crunch Salad ········· 58
Easy Cobb Salad ········· 58
Egg Salad And Toast Points ········· 59
Grainy Mustard-Potato Salad ········· 59
Honey-Lime Fruit Salad ········· 60
Nutty Parmesan-Kale Salad ········· 60
Orzo Pesto Salad ········· 61
Shaved Brussels Sprouts Salad ········· 61

Chapter 8: Sandwich, Brownies & Tarts ·································· 63

Blackened Tuna Sandwiches ···················· 63

Cheesy Egg Sandwich ························· 63

Chicken Skewer Sandwiches ···················· 64

Lemon-Blueberry Shortbread Tart ············· 64

German Chocolate Brownies ···················· 65

Mini Orange Cookie Tarts ······················ 65

Strawberry-Rhubarb Mini Tarts ···················· 66

Rocky Road Brownies ························· 67

Chocolate-Pomegranate Brownies ·············· 67

Chapter 9: Pies ·································· 69

Tender Banana Cream Pie ···················· 69

Black-Bottom Chocolate Cream Pie ············· 70

Caramel Apple Streusel Pie ···················· 70

Creamy Mango Pie ························· 71

Little Chicken And Mushroom Biscuit Pot Pies ·· 71

Double-Crust Blueberry Pie ························· 72

Peachy Pecan Crumb Pie ···················· 72

Old-Fashioned Strawberry Pie ···················· 73

Southern Chocolate Walnut Pie ················ 73

Mini Pot Pies ································· 74

Conclusion ·································· 76

Introduction

Hey, kiddos! You are here, right? That means cooking in your kitchen is something that you definitely enjoy. Well, it is a healthy hobby, I must say. Nothing can satisfy you more than making your favourite treat or snack all by yourself. Yes, some recipes may seem difficult for now, as you are just starting to work your way around the kitchen. I still remember the time I used to bake rock-hard cookies and gooey cakes- well, that's all a part of learning. You try, you make mistakes, and eventually, you become good at it. For me, it was my mom's easy home recipes that she listed, especially for me to start my culinary experience as a young chef. And I thought, why not share some easy, quick and delicious recipes with you all through this cookbook. So, let's get started!

Chapter 1: Welcome to Culinary School

You are about to step into your first-ever culinary class! Things will get exciting from here on. You will have to put on your apron, pick your favourite recipe, gather all the ingredients, select the right tools and then get started with creating the magic of flavours. But before you get your hands on anything, let me take you on a little tour of a kitchen and tell you what you will have there that can help you become the chef you want to be:

Inside a Chef's Kitchen

The kitchen, the heart of every home and the place that pulls you towards it every time you smell your mom baking a pizza or any of your favourite meals, is full of tools, appliances and utensils. Since you are new to the whole cooking experience, you will have to start with some basic kitchen tools, and as you will advance in your cooking skills, you can start using other utensils as well- but only under the supervision of any adult.

Tools and Utensils

Colander: A basket with holes to strain the liquid out of veggies, fruits or pasta etc

Measuring Cups: Marked cups with different sizes to measure different ingredients.

Ice-pop Molds:Plastic or silicon containers to freeze ice-pops.

Measure spoons: Marked spoons with different sizes to measure different ingredients.

Knives: Sharp edged utensils to cut food.

Meat thermometer: Used to read the internal temperature of meat during cooking.

Ladle: A deep-mouthed spoon to pour out soup and other liquids.

Melon Baller: A small scoop to cut the flesh of melon or other fruits into balls.

 **Mortar and pestle:** A heavy bowl with a hand grinder to mesh spices and herbs etc.

 **Spatula:** A flat mouthed spoon used to flip pancakes or mix batters evenly.

 **Parchment paper:** A paper that is placed under food to prevent it from sticking during cooking.

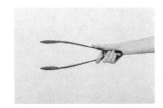 **Tongs:** Used to pick and handle food items.

 **Pastry brush:** A brush with silicone bristle to apply a thin layer of oil, beaten egg or glaze over food.

 **Vegetable peeler:** Used to peel vegetables and fruits.

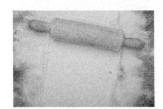 **Rolling pin:** A tool used to spread and roll out the dough into thin sheets.

 **Whisk:** A hand tool used to mix batters to make them lump-free

 **Skewers:** Long sticks used to thread meat, vegetables or fruits for grilling.

 **Zester or box grater:** A tool with uneven and sharp or bladed surfaces to grate lemon peel or cheeses etc.

Cookware

 **Cast iron saucepan:** A deep and heavy-based iron cookware that is used for cooking soups, stews, curries and other liquids.

 **Frying pan:** A slightly less deeper and broader pan with a handle. It is available in different sizes as well.

Grill pan: A pan with a grilling surface.

Steamer basket: A steel basket with holes at the base. It is placed on top of boiling water inside a large cooking pot to steam food.

Saucepan: A deep pan with a handle and a lid. It comes in different sizes to cook desired amount of food.

Bakeware

Baking Dish: A 5 – 10 cm deep pan with varying sizes, is used for cooking things in the oven.

Ramekins: Differently sized cups made out of porcelain or silicone to bake things.

Baking sheet: A oven-proof sheet with or without a rim, available in different sizes.

Roasting pan: A shallow pan used to roast turkey, chicken or other meat or vegetables in the oven.

Muffin pans: A baking pan with muffin cups in it.

Springform pan: A baking pan with removable walls. Mostly it is used for baking cakes.

Pizza Stone: A stone base, which is heated in the oven to cook pizza base or flatbread.

Wire cooling rack: A rack used to cook cookies, cakes and other baked goods.

Kitchen Appliances

Blender: An electric machine with a jug with a blade at its base. It is used to blend food.

Toaster oven: An electric appliance to toast bread or to bake things like an oven.

Microwave: It is only used for heating, melting or defrosting food.

Hand blender: An electric handheld blender that can be inserted into the hot soups or other food to blend.

Stand mixer: A mixer with a mixing bowl and detachable mixing tools.

Food processor: An electric appliance with different rotating blades to mix, blend or process food for cooking.

Oven: A rectangular appliance with a heat-able space inside for cooking. An oven can run on gas, or electricity.

How To Become a Good Chef?

If you are planning to be a young chef at home, then there are certain culinary principles that you will have to stick to. These rules will make cooking an easy and fun experience for you:

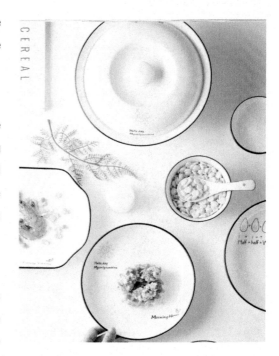

·Know your Recipes

You don't have to rush anything up. Take your time, read the instructions of every recipe carefully and read it again if anything does not make sense to you. Look out for the ingredients and ask any adult in the house to help you understand your recipe if needed. You should know your recipes well before you practically start making anything.

·Prepare your Ingredients Ahead:

Everything get much easier when you have all your ingredients ready before cooking. If the vegetables and fruits need to be cut, then do it before you start putting things together. Keep everything ready in different bowls so that during cooking, you will only have to concentrate on adding them to the cookware.

·Clean while cooking:

"I will clean this later" this thought often comes to mind when you are working in the kitchen, but it's not wise to leave everything to be cleaned later; that only adds an extra burden of work on you. Plus, leaving things around in the kitchen to be cleaned up later only increase the mess, and that can keep you distracted from good cooking. So it is best to clean everything right and there. Divide the whole task of cooking your recipe into different milestones.

First, focus on preparing the ingredients, then wash the things used in the process and keep the things aside. Clean the counter, then move to the next step. Add the cleaning steps in between the different parts of cooking. In this way, you will have nothing to do at the end, and you can sit at the table to enjoy your food while being tension-free.

·Keep things organized:

When you are cooking, you have to add different ingredients at the right time, and you can not do that if everything is not organized. When you start cooking, keep the ingredients on the counter ready to be added in the right order.

·Taste As you cook:

Our taste buds help us the most while cooking. After you add spices or seasonings to the food, you should taste it. Start by adding a small amount of spices or seasonings so that you can add more later. Do not add too many seasonings at a time, especially if you are not sure of the amount. Try to use the measuring spoons to add the exact amount suggested in the recipe.

·Keep a Close Eye:

Cooking needs attention! If you have a video game to play, then don't do it while your pasta boils. Leaving things cooking on the stove is dangerous; sometimes food gets burnt or overcooked, which wastes your ingredients, time and effort. So stay in the kitchen, keep your eyes on the things cooking on the stove or inside the oven.

·Learn from others:

Seeing your mom or dad making batters, doughs or sauces in the kitchen helps you learn a lot of different techniques. So, stand there while your parents are in the kitchen; they may also give you great tips about handling different ingredients.

·Take caution

While handling hot cookware, always use hand mittens. Maintain a safe distance from the food cooking on the stove. Avoid licking food from the hot pot while it's cooking. Let the food cool down a bit before you taste it. Be careful while using knives and forks; keep your fingers and face-especially your eyes, protected. Do not leave the stove on when you are done cooking. Always switch off the oven or other appliances after you are done using them.

All About the Ingredients

Cooking is all about putting the right ingredients together, and how can you do so? By bringing those ingredients home! So next time you decide to bake mini muffins or a chocolate cake in your kitchen, then make sure to get the required ingredients on your trip to the grocery store with your parents and then keep them ready in the pantry to start cooking:

·Dairy

Dairy includes all the food items besides meat that are sourced from animals. Following ingredients make the list of dairy products that you can use in your recipes:

* Whole Milk	* Low fat milk	* Eggs	* Buttermilk
* Feta Cheese	* Cream cheese	* Heavy Cream	* Butter
* Mozzarella cheese	* Cheddar cheese	* Gruyere cheese	* Haloumi cheese
* Ricotta cheese etc			

Most dairy products require refrigeration or freezing for storage, so make sure to keep them in your refrigerator or freezer until you are ready to use them.

·Flour

Flour is the powdered form of grain and some legumes. It comes in different varieties, and it is used in different baked and fried dishes. The most commonly used flours include:

* Plain flour	* Bread flour	* Whole-wheat flour	* Almond flour
* Coconut flour			

For usual baking or cooking, you can use plain or whole-wheat flour.

·Fruits

Fruits are used in a variety of smoothies, desserts and salads. You can get canned, fresh or frozen fruits for your recipes. But remember, fruits have a short shelf-life, and they go bad quickly, so use them soon or keep them refrigerated until you are ready to use them. Some fruits that are commonly used in cooking include:

* Avocado	* Bananas	* Apples	* Blueberries
* Strawberries	* Cranberries	* Peaches	* Oranges
* Pears and peaches	* Pineapples		

Fruits are a great source of fibre and vitamins, so try to add them to your meals more.

·Grains

Rice, wheat, barley, quinoa etc., are different types of grains that are used in our recipes. The dried grains are stored in a container in the pantry, and they are boiled in hot liquid for eating.

·Herbs

Herbs are the edible green leaves that are added to the food to give it a good taste and aroma. Following herbs are used in our meals in both the dried and fresh forms. The dried herbs can be stored at room temperature in a sealed bottle, whereas the fresh ones have to be stored in the refrigerator in a sealed container.

* Coriander	* Parsley	* Basil	* Thyme
* Rosemary	* Oregano	* Mint	

·Legumes

Lentils, peas, peanuts, and beans are all part of this group, and they are used in salads, soups, stews and other main dishes. The legumes you can stock in your pantry include:

* Black beans	* Kidney beans	* Cannellini beans	* Chickpeas

Canned beans and chickpeas are easier to use as they are already cooked. You just need to drain and use them in the recipes.

Nuts and Seeds

Nuts and seeds make a healthy addition to the food. They are added to desserts, breakfast, snacks and smoothies. The nuts and seeds that are good for you include:

* Almonds	* Pine nuts	* Hazelnuts	* Sunflower seeds
* Chia seeds etc			

Oils

Oils are used for all sorts of cooking. There is a variety of oils and fats that are used in the kitchen; the healthier options include:

* Olive oil	* Coconut oil	* Rapeseed oil

·Pasta

Pasta always saves the day- you can cook it in great variety, and it tastes amazing every time. There are different shapes available in pasta. You can bring any depending upon the type of meals you are going to make with it. You can get:

* Penne pasta
* Fettuccini
* Rigatoni
* Elbow macaroni
* Bow tie pasta
* Linguine pasta
* Spaghetti noodles etc.

Pasta comes in dried form; you need to boil them first to use in the recipe. Follow the instruction on the box of the pasta to cook them.

·Spices

Spices add flavour to the food, and there are tons of spices that we use in our dishes. Mostly the spices are available in powdered forms, such as:

* Black pepper
* Salt
* Cayenne pepper
* Paprika
* Turmeric
* White pepper* Nutmeg
* Cinnamon etc

·Sweeteners:

Any edible food product that adds sweetness to the food is called a sweetener. The most commonly used sweeteners include:

* Granulated or icing sugar.
* Brown sugar
* White sugar
* Honey
* Maple syrup

·Vegetables

Cooking is not possible without the use of vegetables. In almost every main dish, a vegetable is used. Fresh and frozen vegetables are a great source of energy and fibre. The main categories of vegetables that you can get for your meals include:

* Alliums: Garlic, onion, scallion, chives, leeks
* Tubers: potato, sweet potato, beets, yams, yellow squash
* Greens: spinach, cabbage, lettuce, Swiss chard, rocket, kale, mustard greens etc.
* Others: cauliflower, broccoli, tomato, carrots, radishes, turnip, etc

·Sauces and Vinegar

They make up a separate group of food that is used to add flavour to the recipes. You can buy sauces and vinegar from the grocery store to add to your dishes.

* Apple cider vinegar
* White vinegar
* Rice vinegar
* Tomato sauce
* BBQ sauce
* Worcestershire sauce
* Soy sauce
* Fish sauce
* Hot sauce

Serving tips

A good garnishing can make your dish look irresistible to all. Different dishes are garnished differently to give them a good look. Here are some of the ingredients that are used to garnish different types of meals:

1.For Smoothies

* Chopped nuts
* Berries
* Coconut shreds
* Whipped cream
* Slice fruits

2.For Pancakes and porridges

* Maple syrup
* Chocolate syrup
* Berries
* Honey
* Chopped canned or fresh fruits

3.For Sweets and desserts

* Icing sugar or sweeteners
* Chocolate syrup
* Cream frosting
* Sweet glaze
* Caramel sauce
* Maple Syrup
* Honey
* Fruits
* Jelly

4.For Stews, soups and curries

* Chopped coriander
* Chopped chilies
* Tortilla chips
* Grated cheese
* A dollop of cream
* Mint leaves
* Basil leaves

Those are just some basic ideas to style your dish for serving. You can get as creative as you want to be. Just pick the right size of the serving dish, place a suitable spoon, or spatula in the food for serving and garnish it according to the flavours of the meal. Then serve and dig in!

Setting Up the table

A pro homechef knows his or her way around setting the table. It is like the last yet the most important act of a play. If a table is set right, it can give the people on the table a great eating experience. So let me tell you here what type of things you will need to set your dinner table, and then I will share a step by step guide to do so.

Things You Will Need:

The following things are listed for one person setting, so if there are more people expected to eat on the table, then set the plates and glasses for each in the same manner. Here is what you need to set per person:

* Table runners and mats
* A dinner plate
* A bread plate
* A drinking cup
* A napkin
* A fork
* A spoon
* A table knife

Ask any adult in your house; he or she will tell you where to get those things in the kitchen. You can then bring them to the dinner table.

Step 01: Place the runners and Mats

First, start by placing a table runner on the table in front of each chair. These runners or mats are important as they keep the table underneath them clean while you eat. For a dinner table, there is one large runner that is placed at the centre of the table, on which you place the main dishes to serve. Then there are small runners for each serving. If you have a six-person table, then you will have to put one small runner for each person on the table.

Step 02: Set the Dinner Plates

Now it is time to set the plates. Start by placing the dinner plate for each person. Imagine you are sitting on the dinner table's chair, then you will have put the dinner plate exactly in front of you on the runner.

Step 03: Place the Bread plate

Raise your left hand, and join the tips of your index finger and thumb to make an "O" and keep the rest of the finger-pointing upwards. What do you see? You just made a "b" out of your left hand. The bread plate starts from "b", so you will place it on the left-hand side of the dinner plate.

Step 04: Set the drinking cup

Raise your right hand, and join the tips of your index finger and thumb to make an "O" and keep the rest of the finger-pointing upwards. What do you see? You just made a "d" out of your right hand. The drinking cup starts from "d", so you will place it on the left-hand side of the dinner plate.

Step 05: Arrange the Napkin

The napkin is used to cover the lap or your clothes when you are eating. It is placed on one side of the dinner plate from where a person can pick it up easily and unfold it to spread on his or her lap. First, you should fold the napkin four times then place it on the "RIGHT" side of the dinner plate. While eating, you use the napkin and afterwards, the napkin is placed on the "LEFT" hand side of the dinner plate.

Step 06: Arrange the Fork

How many letters are there in the word "Fork"? There are four letters, right? And how many letters are there in the word "Left"- there are also four-letters in this word? That means you should put the fork on the left-hand side of the dinner table.

Step 07: Place the Spoon and Knife

Now count with me the number of letters in the words "spoon" and "knife"- there are five letters in both words. Amazingly there are five letters in the word "right", so you will have to put the spoon and the knife on the right-hand side of the dinner table, on top of the napkin that has been already placed there.

Chapter 2: Cakes & Cupcakes

Angel Food Cake

Prep Time: 50 minutes, Cook Time: 45 minutes, Serves:1 cake (serves 12)

INGREDIENTS:

190 g icing sugar, sifted   125 g plain flour, sifted

365 g egg whites (from 10 to 12 large eggs)

1½ teaspoons cream of tartar

1 teaspoon vanilla extract   200 g granulated sugar

TOOLS/EQUIPMENT:

Medium bowl   Large bowl

Stand mixer with whisk attachment or electric hand mixer

Sieve (or mesh strainer)

25 cm tube pan (with removable bottom)

Wire rack or sturdy glass bottle

DIRECTIONS:

1. Preheat the oven to 175˚C.
2. First, make sure the oven rack is in the lowest position.
3. Combine the sugar and flour.
4. In a medium bowl, mix together the icing sugar and flour until well blended with no lumps.
5. In a large bowl, add the egg whites, cream of tartar, and vanilla. Beat on medium until the whites start getting foamy, 1 to 2 minutes. Increase the speed to medium-high, and continue beating until the egg whites become thick and opaque, 1 to 2 minutes.
6. With the mixer on medium-high speed, slowly add the granulated sugar, 1 to 2 tablespoons at a time. Continue beating until the egg whites are shiny and stiff peaks form, 4 to 6 minutes.
7. Gently sift about a quarter of the flour and icing sugar mixture over the egg whites. Very gently fold in the flour mixture with a large rubber spatula, being careful to not deflate the egg whites. Repeat with the remaining flour and icing sugar until just folded in.
8. Pour the batter into an ungreased 25 cm tube pan. Lightly run a butter knife through the batter to remove any air bubbles. Bake for 35 to 45 minutes, or until the top is lightly browned and springs back when lightly touched. Set the cake upside down over a wire rack or sturdy glass bottle to cool. When cooled, run a butter knife around the edge to loosen before inverting onto a plate.

Banana Coffee Cake

Prep Time: 10 minutes, Cook Time: 50 minutes, Serves:6

INGREDIENTS:

FOR THE CAKE

Nonstick cooking spray   250 g plain flour

2½ tablespoons baking powder

½ teaspoon salt   3 overripe bananas

400 g granulated sugar 240 ml whole milk

115 g melted and cooled butter

2 large eggs   1 teaspoon vanilla extract

FOR THE CRUMB TOPPING

150 g brown sugar   180 g plain flour

6 tablespoons cold butter, cut into 12 pieces

TOOLS/EQUIPMENT:

Cutting board   Knife

13-by-23 cm baking dish

1 small, 1 large, and 1 medium bowl

Whisk   Potato masher

Pastry cutter (optional) Toothpick

DIRECTIONS:

1. Preheat the oven to 175°C. Spray a 33-by-23 -cm baking dish with cooking spray. Set aside.
2. In a small bowl, whisk together the flour, baking powder, and salt. Set aside.
3. In a large bowl, mash the bananas with a potato masher until mushy. Add the granulated sugar, milk, butter, eggs, and vanilla, and stir until fully combined. Add the flour mixture, and mix until fully combined. Scrape the batter into the prepared baking dish.
4. In a medium bowl, combine the brown sugar, flour, and butter. Using a pastry cutter or your fingertips, blend until the mixture resembles crumbs. Sprinkle the topping over the batter.
5. Bake for 45 to 50 minutes, or until a toothpick inserted into the middle comes out dry. Allow the cake to cool, then cut into squares and serve.

Chocolate Layer Cake

Prep Time: 45 minutes, Cook Time: 1 hour 15 minutes (plus cooling), Serves:16

INGREDIENTS:

CAKE LAYERS

250 g plain flour

85 g unsweetened cocoa

1½ teaspoons baking soda

¼ teaspoon salt

185 g butter, softened, plus more for greasing the pan

200 g packed brown sugar   200 g granulated sugar

3 large eggs   2 teaspoons vanilla extract

360 ml low-fat buttermilk

FROSTING

30 g unsweetened cocoa   230 g butter, softened

2 tablespoons icing sugar

300 gsemisweet chocolate, melted and cooled

DIRECTIONS:

1. Prepare Cake Layers: Preheat oven to 175°C. Grease three 20 cm-round cake pans. Line bottoms with waxed paper; grease paper. Dust pans with flour.

2. In large bowl with wire whisk, mix flour, cocoa, baking soda, and salt. In another large bowl with mixer on low speed, beat butter and sugars until blended. Increase speed to high; beat for 5 minutes or until mixture is pale and fluffy, occasionally scraping down sides of bowl with rubber spatula. Reduce mixer speed to medium-low; add eggs, 1 at a time, beating well after each addition. Beat in vanilla. Alternately, add flour mixture and buttermilk, beginning and ending with flour mixture, just until smooth, occasionally scraping down sides of bowl with rubber spatula.

3. Spoon batter evenly among prepared cake pans. Bake for 22 to 25 minutes or until toothpick inserted in center of cakes comes out clean. Cool cakes, in pans, on wire racks for 10 minutes. With small knife, loosen cake layers from sides of pans, and turn cake layers over onto wire racks. Carefully remove and discard waxed paper; cool completely, about 45 minutes. Cakes can be made ahead, wrapped tightly in plastic wrap, and stored at room temperature for up to 1 day or frozen for up to 1 month. Bring to room temperature before frosting cake.

4. Prepare Frosting: Meanwhile, in small bowl, mix cocoa and 80 ml boiling water, stirring until smooth. In large bowl, with mixer on medium-high speed, beat butter and icing sugar for 5 minutes or until fluffy. Reduce speed to medium-low; add melted chocolate, then cocoa mixture, beating until smooth and occasionally scraping down sides of bowl with rubber spatula. If frosting is too runny, refrigerate until just stiff enough to spread.

5. Assemble Cake: Place 1 cake layer, bottom side up, on cake plate; spread with ⅓ frosting. Top with second layer, bottom side up; spread with ⅓ frosting. Place remaining layer, bottom side up, on top. Spread remaining frosting over sides and top of cake.

Epic Pound Cake

Prep Time: 15 minutes, Cook Time: 1 hour 20 minutes (plus cooling), Serves:10

INGREDIENTS:

185 g plain flour   ¼ teaspoon baking soda

¼ teaspoon salt   200 g granulated sugar

115 g butter, softened

100 g cream cheese, softened

1 teaspoon freshly grated lemon peel

3 large eggs, at room temperature

2 teaspoons vanilla extract

DIRECTIONS:

1. Preheat oven to 160°C. Grease 22 x 11 cm loaf pan, and dust lightly with flour.

2. In large bowl with wire whisk, mix flour, baking soda, and salt. In another large bowl, with mixer on medium speed, beat sugar, butter, cream cheese, and lemon peel until smooth. Beat in eggs, 1 at a time, occasionally scraping down sides of bowl with rubber spatula. Beat in vanilla. In 2 batches, beat in flour mixture until just combined.

3. Scoop batter into prepared loaf pan; smooth top. Bake for 1 hour 5 minutes to 1 hour 10 minutes or until toothpick inserted in center of cake comes out clean. Cool cake, in pan, for 10 minutes on wire rack. Remove cake from pan and cool completely on wire rack.

Cinnamon Nut Coffee Cake

Prep Time: 30 minutes, Cook Time: 60 minutes, Serves:1 cake (serves 16)

INGREDIENTS:

FOR THE FILLING

100 g granulated sugar

120 g chopped walnuts or pecans

1½ teaspoons cinnamon

FOR THE CAKE

280 g plain flour   2 teaspoons baking powder

½ teaspoon baking soda   ¼ teaspoon table salt

75 g unsalted butter, at room temperature

200 g granulated sugar 80 ml vegetable or rapeseed

oil

2 large eggs, at room temperature

2 teaspoons vanilla extract

240 g sour cream or plain Greek yogurt

TOOLS/EQUIPMENT:

25 cm tube pan (with removable bottom)Small bowl

2 large bowls   Electric hand mixer or stand mixer

Wire rack   Butter, for greasing the pan

Flour, for dusting the pan

DIRECTIONS:

1. Preheat the oven to 175˚C.
2. Grease and flour a 25 cm tube pan.
3. In a small bowl, mix together 100 g of sugar, the walnuts or pecans, and cinnamon until well combined.
4. In a large bowl, mix the flour, baking powder, baking soda, and salt until well blended.
5. In a separate large bowl, beat the butter with an electric mixer on medium speed for about 10 seconds, or until smooth. Beat in 200 g of sugar and the oil, until well blended and light and fluffy, about 2 minutes. Beat in the eggs, one at a time, beating after each egg is added. Beat in the vanilla, then beat in the sour cream.
6. Slowly beat the butter mixture into the dry ingredients until just blended.
7. Spoon half of the cake batter into the tube pan. Spread with a spoon to form an even layer across the bottom of the pan. Sprinkle half of the nut filling over the batter, then top with the remaining batter.
8. Bake for 45 to 60 minutes, or until a toothpick inserted into the middle comes out clean. Cool slightly, then remove from the pan to cool completely on a wire rack.

Crumb Cake

Prep Time: 25 minutes, Cook Time: 1 hour 5 minutes (plus cooling), Serves:10

INGREDIENTS:

FOR CRUMB TOPPING

55 g pecans, toasted and chopped

70 g packed dark brown sugar   30 g plain flour

½ teaspoon ground cinnamon

2 tablespoons butter

FOR CAKE

180 g plain flour   1 teaspoon baking powder

¼ teaspoon baking soda   ¼ teaspoon salt

175 g granulated sugar   4 tablespoons butter

1 teaspoon vanilla extract   2 large eggs

160 g sour cream

DIRECTIONS:

1. Prepare Crumb Topping: In small bowl, mix pecans, brown sugar, flour, and cinnamon until well blended. With your fingertips, work in softened butter until mixture resembles marbles.
2. Prepare Cake: Preheat oven to 175°C. Grease 23 cm springform pan and dust with flour. In medium bowl with wire whisk, mix flour, baking powder, baking soda, and salt.
3. In large bowl with mixer on medium speed, beat granulated sugar, butter, and vanilla for 5 to 6 minutes or until mixture is light and fluffy, occasionally scraping bowl with rubber spatula. Reduce mixer speed to low; add eggs, 1 at a time, beating well after each addition.
4. With mixer on low speed, alternately add flour mixture and sour cream, beginning and ending with flour mixture, just until smooth, occasionally scraping down side of bowl with rubber spatula.
5. Pour batter into prepared springform pan. Sprinkle evenly with crumb topping and gently press into batter. Bake for 40 to 45 minutes or until toothpick inserted in center of cake comes out clean. Cool cake, in pan, on wire rack. With small metal spatula, loosen cake from side of pan and remove springform ring. Cake can be made ahead, wrapped tightly in plastic wrap, and frozen for up to 1 month.

Gingerbread Cupcakes

Prep Time: 25 minutes, Cook Time: 50 minutes (plus cooling), Serves:2 dozen cupcakes

INGREDIENTS:

375 plain flour   150 g sugar   340 g light (mild) molasses   115 g butter, softened

1 tablespoon ground ginger   2 large eggs   choice of frosting

1½ teaspoons ground cinnamon   Pineapple Flowers, opposite, optional

¾ teaspoon baking soda   ¾ teaspoon salt

DIRECTIONS:

1. Preheat oven to 175°C. Line twenty-four 6 cm muffin-pan cups with paper liners.

2. In large bowl with mixer on low speed, combine flour, sugar, ginger, cinnamon, baking soda, and salt. Add molasses, butter, eggs, and 240 ml water; beat until blended. Increase speed to high; beat for 1 to 2 minutes or until creamy, occasionally scraping down sides of bowl with rubber spatula.

3. Spoon batter into prepared muffin-pan cups, filling each cup about ⅔ full. Bake for 23 to 25 minutes or until toothpick inserted in center of cupcakes comes out clean. Immediately remove cupcakes from pans and cool completely on wire rack.

4. When cupcakes are cooled, spread frosting on top and garnish with Pineapple Flowers, right, if using.

Coconut Explosion Cupcakes

Prep Time: 30 minutes, Cook Time: 20 minutes, Serves:12 cupcakes

INGREDIENTS:

FOR THE CUPCAKES

Butter, for greasing the pan (optional)

Flour, for dusting the pan (optional)

125 g plain flour   ½ teaspoon baking powder

½ teaspoon baking soda   ⅛ teaspoon table salt

50 g shortening, at room temperature

175 g granulated sugar 2 large egg whites

½ teaspoon vanilla extract

½ teaspoon coconut extract

60 g sweetened flaked coconut 160 ml buttermilk

FOR THE FROSTING

1 (200 g brick) cream cheese, at room temperature

6 tablespoons shortening, softened

½ teaspoon coconut extract

375 – 450 g icing sugar

40 g sweetened flaked coconut   Milk

TOOLS/EQUIPMENT:

Muffin pan   Paper liners (optional)

Medium bowl   Large bowl

Electric hand mixer or stand mixer   Wire rack

Spatula

DIRECTIONS:

1. Preheat the oven to 175˚C.

2. Grease and lightly flour a 12-cup muffin pan or line with paper liners.

3. In a medium bowl, stir together the flour, baking powder, baking soda, and salt.

4. In a large bowl, beat 50 g of shortening with an electric mixer on medium speed for about 10 seconds, or until smooth. Beat in the granulated sugar until well blended and light and fluffy, about 2 minutes. Beat in the egg whites, one at a time, beating after each is added. Beat in the vanilla and ½ teaspoon of coconut extract. Fold in 60 g of flaked coconut.

5. Alternate adding the flour mixture and the buttermilk to the shortening mixture, beating on low after each addition until batter is just blended.

6. Spoon the batter into muffin cups about ⅔ full. Bake for 18 to 20 minutes, or until a toothpick inserted into the center comes out clean. Cool slightly, then remove the cupcakes to finish cooling on a wire rack.

7. In a large bowl, beat together the cream cheese and 6 tablespoons of shortening until smooth. Beat in ½ teaspoon of coconut extract. Beat in 250 g of icing sugar, adding more as needed while beating until a spreading consistency. Fold in 40 g of flaked coconut. If the frosting is too thick, you can stir in a little milk, a few teaspoons at a time.

8. When the cupcakes are completely cooled, frost the cupcakes with a spatula.

Golden Butter Cupcakes

Prep Time: 15 minutes, Cook Time: 35 minutes (plus cooling), Serves:2

INGREDIENTS:

250 g plain flour

2½ teaspoons baking powder

180 g butter, softened

300 g sugar

1 teaspoon salt

180 ml whole milk

1½ teaspoons vanilla extract

choice of frosting

3 large eggs

DIRECTIONS:

1. Preheat oven to 175°C. Line twenty-four 6 cm muffin-pan cups with paper liners.

2. In a large bowl with mixer on low speed, mix flour, sugar, baking powder, and salt until combined. Add butter, milk, vanilla, and eggs; beat just until blended. Increase speed to high; beat for 1 to 2 minutes or until creamy, occasionally scraping down sides of bowl with rubber spatula.

3. Spoon batter into prepared muffin-pan cups. Bake for 20 to 25 minutes or until cupcakes are golden brown and toothpick inserted in center of cupcakes comes out clean. Immediately remove cupcakes from pans and cool completely on wire rack.

4. When cupcakes are cool, spread frosting on tops.

Cupcakes With Chocolate Fudge Frosting

Prep Time: 30 minutes, Cook Time: 25 minutes, Serves:12 cupcakes

INGREDIENTS:

FOR THE CAKE

Butter, for greasing the pan (optional)

Flour, for dusting the pan (optional)

125 g plain flour

1 teaspoon baking powder

¼ teaspoon baking soda

¼ teaspoon table salt

75 g unsalted butter, at room temperature

120 g granulated sugar

1½ teaspoons vanilla extract

2 large eggs, at room temperature   80 ml milk

FOR THE FROSTING

75 g unsalted butter

55 g unsweetened cocoa powder

375 g icing sugar   80 ml milk

1 teaspoon vanilla extract

TOOLS/EQUIPMENT:

Muffin pan

Stand mixer (or hand mixer and large bowl)

Medium bowl   Paper liners (optional)

DIRECTIONS:

1. Preheat the oven to 175°C.

2. Grease and lightly flour a 12-cup muffin pan or line with paper liners.

3. In a medium bowl, stir together the flour, baking powder, baking soda, and salt.

4. In a large bowl, beat the butter with an electric mixer on medium speed for about 10 seconds, or until smooth. Beat in the granulated sugar and 1½ teaspoons of vanilla until well blended and light and fluffy, about 2 minutes. Beat in the eggs, one at a time, beating after each egg is added.

5. Alternate adding the flour mixture and the 80 ml milk to the butter mixture, beating on low after adding each, until the batter is just combined.

6. Spoon the batter into muffin cups about ½ full. Bake for 18 to 20 minutes, or until a toothpick inserted into the center comes out clean. Cool slightly, then transfer to a wire rack to finish cooling.

7. In a small saucepan over medium heat, melt the remaining 75 g butter. Add the cocoa powder and bring to a boil, stirring constantly. Pour the mixture into a medium bowl and cool completely. Beat in the icing sugar with the electric mixer on medium speed. Beat in the 80 ml milk, a little at a time, until the frosting is a smooth, spreadable consistency, then beat in 1 teaspoon of vanilla.

8. When cupcakes are completely cooled, frost with a spatula.

Chocolate Fudge Layer Cake with Peanut Butter Frosting

Prep Time: 30 minutes, Cook Time: 30 minutes,

Serves:1 (2-layer) cake

INGREDIENTS:

FOR THE CAKE

Butter, for greasing the pans

Flour, for dusting the pans   250 g plain flour

65 g unsweetened cocoa powder

1 teaspoon baking soda   ¾ teaspoon baking powder

½ teaspoon table salt

185 g unsalted butter, at room temperature

400 g granulated sugar

3 large eggs, at room temperature

2 teaspoons vanilla extract   360 g milk

170 g mini chocolate chips

FOR THE FROSTING

230 g unsalted butter, at room temperature

320 g creamy peanut butter   375 g icing sugar

1 to 2 tablespoons milk

TOOLS/EQUIPMENT:

2 (20 cm) round cake pans   Medium bowl

Large bowl   Electric hand mixer or stand mixer

Wire rack   Offset spatula or butter knife

DIRECTIONS:

1. Preheat the oven to 175°C.
2. Grease and lightly flour 2 (20 cm) round cake pans.
3. In a medium bowl, stir together the flour, cocoa powder, baking soda, baking powder, and salt.
4. In a large bowl, beat butter with an electric mixer on medium speed for about 10 seconds, or until smooth. Beat in the granulated sugar until well blended and light and fluffy, about 2 minutes. Beat in the eggs, one at a time, beating after each egg is added. Beat in the vanilla.
5. Alternate adding the flour mixture and 360 ml of milk to the butter mixture, beating on low after each addition until batter is just combined. Fold in the chocolate chips.
6. Spoon the batter evenly among the 2 prepared cake pans. Bake for 30 to 35 minutes, or until a toothpick inserted into the center comes out clean. Cool slightly, then remove the cakes from the pans to finish cooling on a wire rack.
7. In a large bowl, blend 230 g of butter and the peanut butter with an electric mixer on low speed. Beat in the icing sugar.

Slowly add 1 to 2 tablespoons of milk, beating until the frosting is a spreading consistency.

8. When the cakes are completely cool, place one layer, flat side up, on a serving plate. Spread the frosting over the top with an offset spatula or butter knife. Place the second cake layer on top, flat side down. Spread more frosting on the top and sides of cake as desired.

Dark Chocolate Fudge Lava Cakes

Prep Time: 20 minutes, Cook Time: 12 minutes,

Serves:4 cakes

INGREDIENTS:

Butter, for greasing the ramekins

Flour, for dusting the ramekins

115 g unsalted butter

150 g dark chocolate, chopped

50 g granulated sugar

2 large eggs, at room temperature

2 large egg yolks   ⅛ teaspoon table salt

2 tablespoons plain flour

TOOLS/EQUIPMENT:

4 (150 g) ramekins   Baking sheet

Double boiler   Medium bowl

Electric hand mixer   Spatula

DIRECTIONS:

1. Preheat the oven to 175°C.
2. Grease and lightly flour 4 (150 g) ramekins. Set the ramekins on a baking sheet.
3. Place the butter and the chocolate in the top of a double boiler over boiling water, reduce the heat to low, and mix until smooth. Remove from heat, and cool completely.
4. In a medium bowl, beat the sugar, eggs, egg yolks, and salt with an electric mixer on medium speed until frothy. With a spatula, fold in the cooled chocolate, along with the flour, until just combined.
5. Spoon the batter into the prepared ramekins. Bake for 10 to 12 minutes or until the sides of the cakes look firm but the center still looks a little soft. Cool the cakes for 1 to 2 minutes, then using oven mitts, gently flip them over onto serving plates. Let them sit a few seconds, then wiggle the ramekins slightly to allow the cakes to come out. If the cakes are stuck, gently loosen the edges with a butter knife. Serve immediately.

Dreamy Cheesecake

Prep Time: 20 minutes plus 3 hours to chill, Cook Time: 1 hour, Serves:10

INGREDIENTS:

FOR THE CRUST

½ packet digestive biscuits

1 teaspoon ground cinnamon

3 tablespoons sugar   ½ teaspoon salt

75 g butter, melted

FOR THE CAKE

2 (200 g) packages cream cheese, at room temperature

¼ teaspoon pure vanilla extract

1 teaspoon finely grated lemon zest   250 g sugar

2 tablespoons flour   ¼ teaspoon salt

5 whole eggs, plus 1 egg yolk   60 ml heavy cream

TOOLS / EQUIPMENT

Zester	Resealable bag
Rolling pin	Medium bowl
Rubber spatula	Springform pan
Electric mixer	Large bowl
Small bowl	Baking sheet

DIRECTIONS:

Make the crust.

1. Put the digestive biscuits in a resealable plastic bag. With a rolling pin, crush the biscuits into crumbs. If you prefer a finer crust, continue crushing the biscuits until you've reached a texture you like. In a medium bowl, mix together the crushed biscuits, cinnamon, sugar, and salt. Pour in the melted butter, and stir to combine.

2. Form and set the crust.

3. Use a rubber spatula or the back of a spoon to spread and compress the mixture evenly into a 23 cm springform pan. Press the crust a little up the sides of the pan, ensuring the crust is even at its base and thins as it goes up. Chill in the refrigerator to set while you make the filling.

4. Mix the filling.

5. Preheat the oven to 260°C. In a large bowl, beat the cheese with an electric mixer until fluffy. Add the vanilla and lemon zest, and mix to combine.

6. In a small bowl, stir together the sugar, flour, and salt. Gradually blend the dry ingredients into the cheese. One at a time, add the eggs and additional yolk, whipping to combine

and pausing after each to scrape down the sides of the bowl. Gently incorporate the cream, and whip to combine.

7. Pour the mixture into the crust. Place on a baking sheet, and bake for 5 to 8 minutes. Lower the temperature to 95°C, and bake for about 45 to 55 minutes more, until the edges are golden and the center still jiggles. Turn the oven off, and with the door ajar, allow the cheesecake to cool inside for about an hour. Refrigerate for 3 hours, up to overnight.

8. Remove the cake from the refrigerator. Run a butter knife around the inside edge to loosen the cake from the pan. Open the springform pan, remove the cake, and serve at once.

Mini Almond Flourless Chocolate Cakes

Prep Time: 10 minutes, Cook Time: 30 minutes, Serves:4 cakes

INGREDIENTS:

Butter, for greasing the ramekins

6 tablespoons unsalted butter   85 g honey

110 g dark chocolate chips

95 g finely ground almonds (or almond flour)

2 large eggs, at room temperature, beaten

1 teaspoon vanilla extract   ½ teaspoon table salt

TOOLS/EQUIPMENT:

4 (100 g) ramekins	Baking sheet
Double boiler (or see Make Your Own Double Boiler)	
Medium bowl	Whisk or fork

DIRECTIONS:

1. Preheat the oven to 175°C.

2. Lightly grease 4 small ramekins and place them on a baking sheet.

3. Add the butter, honey, and chocolate chips to the top of a double boiler over boiling water, then reduce the heat to low, mixing until smooth. Set aside to cool completely, about 30 to 45 minutes.

4. In a medium bowl, whisk together the almonds, eggs, vanilla, and salt until well blended. Slowly whisk in the cooled chocolate mixture.

5. Bake for 20 to 30 minutes, or until a toothpick inserted into the middle comes out clean.

Grasshopper Cake Stacks

Prep Time: 30 minutes, Cook Time: 25 minutes,

Serves:15 cakes

INGREDIENTS:

FOR THE CAKES

Butter, for greasing the pans

Flour, for dusting the pans

165 g plain flour

45 g unsweetened cocoa powder

¾ teaspoon baking soda   ½ teaspoon baking powder

¼ teaspoon table salt

115 g unsalted butter, at room temperature

265 g granulated sugar 2 large eggs, at room temperature

1 teaspoon vanilla extract   240 ml milk

FOR THE MINT CHOCOLATE CHIP FROSTING

180 g unsalted butter, at room temperature

1 (400 g) bag icing sugar

2 to 4 tablespoons milk

1 teaspoon mint extract   Green food colouring

260 g finely chopped semisweet chocolate, plus more for garnish (optional)

TOOLS/EQUIPMENT:

2 (23 cm) round cake pans   Medium bowl

Large bowl   Electric hand mixer or stand mixer

Wire rack   5 cm round cookie or biscuit cutter

DIRECTIONS:

1. Preheat the oven to 175˚C.

2. Grease and lightly flour 2 (23 cm) round cake pans.

3. In a medium bowl, stir together the flour, cocoa powder, baking soda, baking powder, and salt.

4. In a large bowl, beat 115 g of butter with an electric mixer on medium speed for about 10 seconds, or until smooth. Beat in the granulated sugar until well blended and light and fluffy, about 2 minutes. Add the eggs, one at a time, beating after each egg is added. Beat in the vanilla.

5. In batches, alternate adding the flour mixture and 240 ml of milk to the butter mixture, beating on low after each addition until the batter is just combined.

6. Spoon the batter evenly between two prepared cake pans. Bake for 20 to 25 minutes, or until a toothpick inserted into the center comes out clean. Cool slightly, then remove the cakes from pans to finish cooling on a wire rack.

7. Using a 5 cm round cookie cutter, cut cake into small rounds. You should get about 15 per pan for a total of 30. Save the cake scraps for other uses.

8. Beat together 180 g of butter and the icing sugar with an electric mixer on medium speed. Slowly add the milk, 1 tablespoon at a time, until it has a frosting consistency. Beat in the mint extract and a few drops of green food colouring until well blended. Add a little more green food colouring as needed to achieve the desired colour. Stir in the chopped chocolate.

9. Spread about 1 tablespoon of frosting over each cake round. Then place one frosted cake round on another to make 15 cakes in total. Garnish with chopped chocolate, if desired.

Rich Chocolate Cupcakes

Prep Time: 15 minutes, Cook Time: 50 minutes (plus cooling), Serves:20

INGREDIENTS:

165 g plain flour   55 g unsweetened cocoa

1½ teaspoons baking powder

½ teaspoon baking soda

½ teaspoon salt   240 ml whole milk

1½ teaspoons vanilla extract   265 g sugar

10 tablespoons butter, softened 2 large eggs

choice of frosting

DIRECTIONS:

1. Preheat oven to 175°C. Line twenty-four 6cm muffin-pan cups with paper liners.

2. In medium bowl with wire whisk, mix flour, cocoa, baking powder, baking soda, and salt. In a liquid measuring cup, mix milk and vanilla.

3. In large bowl with mixer on low speed, beat sugar and butter just until blended. Increase speed to high; beat for 3 minutes or until mixture is light and creamy. Reduce speed to low; add eggs, 1 at a time, beating well after each addition.

4. Add flour mixture, alternately with milk mixture, beginning and ending with flour mixture, just until combined, occasionally scraping down sides of bowl with rubber spatula.

5. Spoon batter into prepared muffin-pan cups, filling each cup about ⅔ full. Bake for 22 to 25 minutes or until toothpick inserted in center of cupcakes comes out clean. Immediately remove cupcakes from pans and cool completely on wire rack.

6. When cupcakes are cool, spread frosting on top.

Lemon Loaf Cake

Prep Time: 20 minutes, Cook Time: 60 minutes,

Serves:1 cake (serves 12)

INGREDIENTS:

FOR THE CAKE

Butter, for greasing the pan

Flour, for dusting the pan   80 ml milk

2 tablespoons freshly squeezed lemon juice

185 g plain flour   ¼ teaspoon baking powder

¼ teaspoon baking soda

¼ teaspoon table salt

115 g unsalted butter, at room temperature

200 g granulated sugar

2 large eggs, at room temperature

½ teaspoon vanilla extract

1 tablespoon freshly grated lemon zest

FOR THE GLAZE

95 g icing sugar

2 teaspoons freshly squeezed lemon juice

1 to 3 tablespoons milk

TOOLS/EQUIPMENT:

Loaf pan	Small bowl
Medium bowl	Large bowl
Electric hand mixer or stand mixer	Zester
Wire rack	Whisk (or fork)

DIRECTIONS:

1. Preheat the oven to 175˚C.
2. Grease and lightly flour a loaf pan.
3. In a small bowl, add 80 ml of milk and 2 tablespoons of lemon juice, and stir to combine. Let sit about 10 minutes.
4. In a medium bowl, stir together the flour, baking powder, baking soda, and salt.
5. In a large bowl, beat the butter with an electric mixer on medium speed for about 10 seconds, or until smooth. Beat in the granulated sugar until well blended and light and fluffy, about 2 minutes. Beat in the eggs, one at a time, beating after each egg is added. Beat in the vanilla and lemon zest.
6. Alternate adding the flour mixture and the milk mixture to the butter mixture, beating on low after each addition, until the batter is just combined.
7. Pour the cake batter into the prepared pan. Bake for 45 to 60 minutes, or until a toothpick inserted into the middle comes out clean. Cool slightly, then remove the cake from the pan to finish cooling on a wire rack.
8. In a medium bowl, whisk together the icing sugar, 2 teaspoons of lemon juice, and 1 tablespoon of milk. Whisk in more milk as needed until thick but spreadable. Spoon the glaze over the top of the cake, so it can drizzle down the sides.

Orange Vanilla Pound Cake

Prep Time: 30 minutes, Cook Time: 90 minutes,

Serves:1 cake (serves 16)

INGREDIENTS:

FOR THE CAKE

Butter, for greasing the pan

Flour, for dusting the pan

375 g plain flour   ½ teaspoon baking powder

½ teaspoon table salt

330 g unsalted butter, at room temperature

600 g granulated sugar

5 large eggs, at room temperature

2 tablespoons freshly grated orange zest

2 teaspoons vanilla extract   240 ml milk

FOR THE ORANGE GLAZE

100 g granulated sugar

120 ml freshly squeezed orange juice (from 2 or 3 oranges)

TOOLS/EQUIPMENT:

1 (25 cm) tube pan	Large bowl
Electric hand mixer or stand mixer	Zester
Small saucepan	Pastry brush

DIRECTIONS:

1. Preheat the oven to 175˚C.
2. Grease and flour a 25 cm tube pan.
3. In a large bowl, combine the flour, baking powder, and salt until well combined.
4. In a separate large bowl, beat the butter with an electric mixer on medium speed until smooth, about 10 seconds. Beat in 600 g of sugar until well blended and light and fluffy, about 2 minutes. Beat in the eggs, one at a time, then beat in the orange zest and vanilla until blended.
5. Alternate beating in the dry ingredients and the milk into the butter mixture until just combined.
6. Pour the batter into the tube pan. Bake for 60 to 90 minutes, or until a toothpick inserted into the middle comes out clean.
7. In a small saucepan over medium heat, heat 100 g of sugar and orange juice, stirring until slightly thickened, about 5 minutes. Brush the glaze over the top and sides of the warm cake.

New York–Style Cheesecake

Prep Time: 30 MINUTES, Cook Time: 1 HOUR 35 MINUTES (PLUS COOLING AND CHILLING),

Serves:16

INGREDIENTS:

Digestive Biscuit–CRUMB CRUST

11 digestive biscuits   4 tablespoons butter, melted

1 tablespoon sugar

CHEESECAKE

3 packages (200 g each) cream cheese, softened

150 g sugar   1 tablespoon flour

1½ teaspoons vanilla extract   3 large eggs

1 large egg yolk   60 ml milk

fresh berries, for garnish, optional

DIRECTIONS:

1. Prepare Crust: Preheat oven to 190°C. In 23 cm springform pan, with fork, mix digestive biscuit crumbs, melted butter, and sugar until crumbs are evenly moistened. Press crumb mixture firmly into bottom and up side of prepared springform pan. Bake for 10 minutes; cool crust, in pan, on wire rack. Reduce oven temperature to 150°C.

2. Prepare Cheesecake: In large bowl with mixer on medium speed, beat cream cheese and sugar until smooth and fluffy. Beat in flour and vanilla until well combined. Reduce speed to low; beat in eggs and egg yolk, 1 at a time, beating well after each addition. Beat in milk just until blended.

3. Pour batter onto prepared crust. Bake for 55 to 60 minutes or until set but still slightly jiggly and moist in center, and pale gold near edge.

4. Cool cheesecake completely, in pan, on wire rack. Refrigerate overnight before serving. With small metal spatula, loosen cake from side of pan and remove springform ring. Garnish with fresh berries, if using.

Pick-Your-Flavour Ice Cream Cake

Prep Time: 30 minutes (plus 1 to 2 hours freezing time), Cook Time: 25 minutes, Serves:1 cake (serves 16)

INGREDIENTS:

FOR THE CAKE

Butter, for greasing the pans   Flour, for dusting the pans

185 g plain flour   45 g unsweetened cocoa powder

1 teaspoon baking powder

¼ teaspoon baking soda

175 g granulated sugar   100 g brown sugar

180 g unsalted butter, melted and cooled

2 large eggs, at room temperature

1 teaspoon vanilla extract   240 ml milk

960 g ice cream, any flavour

FOR THE CHOCOLATE TOPPING

170 g semisweet chocolate chips

2 teaspoons corn syrup

120 g heavy whipping cream

TOOLS/EQUIPMENT:

2 (23 cm) cake pans   Medium bowl

Large bowl   Wire rack

Small saucepan

DIRECTIONS:

1. Preheat the oven to 175˚C.

2. Grease and lightly flour 2 (23 cm) round cake pans.

3. In a medium bowl, mix together the flour, cocoa powder, baking powder, and baking soda until well blended.

4. In a large bowl, mix the granulated sugar, brown sugar, and butter until well blended, about 2 minutes. Add the eggs one at time, beating after each addition, then beat in the vanilla.

5. Alternate beating in the dry ingredients and the milk to the wet ingredients until just combined.

6. Pour the batter evenly into the 2 prepared pans. Bake for 20 to 25 minutes, or until a toothpick inserted into the middle comes out clean. Cool slightly, then remove from pans and place on a wire rack to cool completely.

7. Let the ice cream sit on the counter for 5 to 10 minutes, until soft but not soupy. Place the bottom cake layer, flat side up, on a serving plate. Spoon the ice cream on top of the bottom cake layer, and spread the ice cream to the edge of the cake with a spoon. Top with the other cake layer, flat side down, and press gently on the cake to help spread the ice cream to the edges. Place the cake in the freezer for 1 to 2 hours, or until firm.

8. In a medium bowl, add the chocolate chips and corn syrup. In a small saucepan over low heat, heat the heavy cream, whisking continuously, until it just starts to boil. Pour the hot cream over the chocolate chips. Let sit about 1 minute, then stir to combine until smooth. Let cool.

9. Spoon the cooled chocolate over the top of the cake and let it drip down the sides of the cake. Return the cake to the freezer until ready to serve, at least a half hour. Let the cake sit at room temperature for 10 to 20 minutes to soften before slicing and serving.

Upside-Down Apple Cupcakes

Prep Time: 30 minutes, Cook Time: 20 minutes,

Serves:18 cupcakes

INGREDIENTS:

FOR THE APPLES

4 tablespoons unsalted butter   135 g brown sugar

2 large apples, cored, peeled, and very thinly sliced

FOR THE CAKES

125 g plain flour   1¼ teaspoons baking powder

½ teaspoon cinnamon   ¼ teaspoon table salt

115 g unsalted butter, at room temperature

200 g granulated sugar   1 large egg

1 teaspoon vanilla extract   60 ml buttermilk

TOOLS/EQUIPMENT:

2 muffin pans   Medium frying pan

Medium bowl   Large bowl

Electric mixer   Butter, for greasing the pans

DIRECTIONS:

1. Preheat the oven to 175°C.
2. Generously grease 18 cups of 2 (12-cup) muffin pans.
3. In a medium frying pan over medium heat, heat 4 tablespoons of butter and the brown sugar, stirring until combined and melted. Add the apples, stirring to combine, and cook for 4 to 5 minutes or until the apples are soft, stirring occasionally. Spoon 2 or 3 apple slices and a little sauce into the bottom of each muffin cup.
4. In a medium bowl, stir together the flour, baking powder, cinnamon, and salt.
5. In a large bowl, beat 115 g of room-temperature butter with an electric mixer on medium speed for about 10 seconds, or until smooth. Beat in the granulated sugar until well blended and light and fluffy, about 2 minutes. Add the eggs, one at a time, beating after each egg is added, then beat in the vanilla.
6. In batches, alternate adding the flour mixture and the buttermilk to the butter mixture, beating on low after each addition until the batter is just combined.
7. Spoon the batter over the apples in the muffin cups until half to ⅔ full. Bake for 18 to 20 minutes, or until a toothpick inserted into the center comes out clean. Cool slightly, then gently flip the cakes over onto a platter or serving plate.

Zebra Marble Cake with Vanilla Frosting

Prep Time: 30 minutes, Cook Time: 45 minutes,

Serves:1 cake (serves 8)

INGREDIENTS:

FOR THE CAKE

Butter, for greasing the pan

Flour, for dusting the pan

250 g plain flour   2 teaspoons baking powder

¼ teaspoon table salt   200 g granulated sugar

4 large eggs, at room temperature

240 ml vegetable or rapeseed oil

240 ml milk   1 teaspoon vanilla extract

3 tablespoons sifted unsweetened cocoa powder

FOR THE FROSTING

115 g butter, at room temperature

220 g icing sugar   ½ teaspoon vanilla extract

⅛ teaspoon table salt   3 to 5 tablespoons milk

TOOLS/EQUIPMENT:

1 (23 cm) round cake pan   Medium bowl

Large bowl   Electric hand mixer or stand mixer

Whisk or fork   Wire rack

DIRECTIONS:

1. Preheat the oven to 175°C.
2. Grease and flour a 23 cm round cake pan.
3. In a medium bowl, stir together the flour, baking powder, and ¼ teaspoon of salt.
4. In a large bowl, beat together the granulated sugar and eggs with an electric mixer on medium until well blended, about 2 minutes. Add the oil, 240 ml of milk, and 1 teaspoon of vanilla, beating until well blended.
5. Add the flour mixture to the egg mixture, beating on medium until just blended.
6. Spoon half of the batter into a separate bowl. Whisk the cocoa powder into one of the bowls, stirring to blend.
7. To make stripes, alternate adding the two batters to the pan. Spoon about 3 tablespoons of vanilla batter into the center of the pan. Then spoon about 3 tablespoons of chocolate batter in the middle of the pan on top of the vanilla batter. Repeat until all the batter is in the pan. The cake batter will spread to the edge of the pan as you add more.
8. Bake for 30 to 45 minutes, or until a toothpick inserted into the middle comes out clean. Let the cake cool slightly in the pan, then remove from the pan and place on a wire rack to finish cooling.
9. In a medium bowl, beat together the butter and icing sugar with an electric mixer on medium speed. Beat in ½ teaspoon of vanilla and ⅛ teaspoon of salt. Add a little milk if necessary to thin the frosting. Spread the frosting over the cooled cake

Sprinkle Cake Pops

Prep Time: 60 minutes (plus 1 hour chill time), Cook Time: 25 minutes, Serves:24 cake pops

INGREDIENTS:
FOR THE CAKE

Butter, for greasing the pan

Flour, for dusting the pan

125 g plain flour   1 teaspoon baking powder

¼ teaspoon baking soda   ¼ teaspoon table salt

75 g unsalted butter, at room temperature

130 g granulated sugar

2 large eggs, at room temperature

1½ teaspoons vanilla extract   80 ml milk

TOOLS/EQUIPMENT:

23 cm round cake pan   Medium bowl

Large bowl   Electric stand or hand mixer

Wire rack   Baking sheet

Wax or parchment paper

Double boiler (or see Make Your Own Double Boiler)

Spatula   White lollipop sticks

Cake pop stand, box, or foam

DIRECTIONS:

1. Preheat the oven to 175˚C.

2. Grease and lightly flour a 23 cm round cake pan.

3. In a medium bowl, stir together the flour, baking powder, baking soda, and salt.

4. In a large bowl, beat 75 g of room-temperature butter with an electric mixer on medium speed for about 10 seconds or until smooth. Beat in the granulated sugar until well combined and light and fluffy, about 2 minutes. Beat in the eggs, one at a time, beating after each egg is added. Beat in the vanilla.

5. Alternate adding some of the flour mixture and 80 ml of milk to the butter mixture, beating on low after each addition, until the batter is just combined.

6. Pour the cake batter into the prepared pan. Bake for 20 to 25 minutes, or until a toothpick inserted into the middle comes out clean. Cool slightly, then remove the cake from the pan to finish cooling on a wire rack.

7. When the cake is completely cooled, prepare the frosting. In a medium bowl, add 4 tablespoons of room-temperature butter and beat with an electric mixer for about 10 seconds, or until smooth. Gradually beat in the icing sugar. Add 2 tablespoons of milk and beat until smooth, adding a little more milk at a time as needed. The frosting should be a little on the thicker side.

8. In a large bowl, crumble the cooled cake into pieces. Add ¼ of frosting. Using a sturdy spatula or large spoon, mix together the cake and frosting. Add a little more frosting at a time until the cake is fully crumbled and the mixture starts to clump together.

9. Scoop the cake mixture out into 2.5 cm balls, roll in your hands if necessary to form a ball, and place on a baking sheet lined with wax or parchment paper. 9.Refrigerate for about 1 hour, or until the cake balls are firm.

10. Place the candy melts in the top of a double boiler. Place over boiling water, then reduce the heat to low. Stir constantly, until the candy melts are melted and smooth. Dip about ½ cm of the tip of a lollipop stick into the melted candy melt, then insert the stick into the cake ball. Dip the cake balls, one at a time, in the candy melts, covering the entire cake ball and just below to the stick. You can pour the melted candy melts into a tall narrow container or glass for easier dipping. Before the candy melt hardens, sprinkle the sprinkles on top of the cake balls. Place the cake pops on a cake pop stand or in foam to stand upright. Repeat with the remaining cake balls.

Chapter 3: Bread & Muffins

Chocolate-Glazed Banana Bread Minis

Prep Time: 15 minutes, Cook Time: 45 minutes (plus cooling and standing), Serves:6 loaves

INGREDIENTS:

250 g plain flour	¾ teaspoon baking soda	100 g granulated sugar
¼ teaspoon salt	450 g mashed very ripe bananas	100 g packed light brown sugar
2 teaspoons vanilla extract	115 g butter, softened	2 large eggs 50 g semisweet chocolate, melted

DIRECTIONS:

1. Preheat oven to 175°C.
2. In medium bowl with wire whisk, mix flour, baking soda, and salt. In another medium bowl, mix bananas and vanilla.
3. In large bowl with mixer on medium speed, beat butter and sugars for 3 minutes or until fluffy. Beat in eggs, 1 at a time. Reduce speed to low; alternately add flour mixture and banana mixture, beginning and ending with flour mixture, just until blended, scraping down side of bowl occasionally with rubber spatula.
4. Divide batter among 6 disposable mini loaf pans. Bake for 30 to 35 minutes or until toothpick inserted in centers of breads comes out clean. Cool breads completely in pans on wire rack.
5. Drizzle cooled breads with melted chocolate; let stand until chocolate sets.

Cranberry-Date-Nut Bread

Prep Time: 25 minutes, Cook Time: 1 hour 40 minutes (plus standing and cooling), Serves:16

INGREDIENTS:

25 0g chopped dates	6 tablespoons butter	½ teaspoon salt 1 large egg, lightly beaten
250 g plain flour	150 g sugar	150 g fresh or frozen cranberries, coarsely chopped
1 teaspoon baking powder	½ teaspoon baking soda	110 g pecans, coarsely chopped

DIRECTIONS:

1. In 2-quart saucepan, heat 240 ml water to boiling over high heat. Remove saucepan from heat; stir in dates and butter. Let stand for 30 minutes or until slightly cooled.
2. Preheat oven to 160°C. Grease 23 x 13 cm loaf pan.
3. In large bowl with wire whisk, mix flour, sugar, baking powder, baking soda, and salt. With fork, stir egg into cooled date mixture. Stir date mixture, cranberries, and pecans into flour mixture just until evenly moistened (do not overmix). Spoon batter into prepared loaf pan and spread evenly.
4. Bake for 1 hour and 15 minutes or until toothpick inserted in center of bread comes out clean. Cool bread in pan on wire rack for 10 minutes. Remove from pan and cool completely on rack. Bread can be made ahead, tightly wrapped in plastic wrap, and frozen for up to 1 month.

Honey Oat Bread

Prep Time: 20 minutes (plus 1 hour for dough to rise), Cook Time: 55 minutes, Serves:2 loaves (serves 24)

INGREDIENTS:

1 (5 g) envelope active dry yeast   60 ml warm water

480 ml milk   4 tablespoons unsalted butter, divided

2 tablespoons honey   1 teaspoon table salt

100 g rolled oats

500 – 625 g flour, plus more to flour the work surface

Butter, for greasing the pans

TOOLS/EQUIPMENT:

Large bowl   Small saucepan

Whisk or spoon   2 loaf pans

Aluminum foil   Pastry brush

Wire rack

DIRECTIONS:

1. In a large bowl, stir together the yeast and warm water. Let sit for about 5 minutes.

2. In a small saucepan over medium heat, add the milk, 3 tablespoons of butter, the honey, and salt. Whisk until the butter has melted and the mixture is blended. Let this mixture cool a bit, then pour into the yeast mixture.

3. Add the oats and 500 g of flour to the yeast mixture, and stir until well blended. Add more flour as needed until a sticky dough forms.

4. Place the dough on a well-floured surface. Knead the dough 6 to 8 minutes, adding flour as necessary, until smooth and elastic.

5. Divide the dough in half, form into two loaves, and place each in a well-greased loaf pan. Cover lightly with plastic wrap and place in a dark, warm, draft-free place to double in size, about 1 hour.

6. Preheat the oven to 175°C.

7. Bake the bread for about 25 minutes, then cover with aluminum foil to prevent further browning. Continue baking for an additional 20 to 30 minutes or until the loaves sound hollow when lightly tapped. Melt the remaining tablespoon of butter and brush it on the tops of the loaves. Cool slightly, then transfer to a wire rack to finish cooling.

Lemon-Glazed Earl Grey Tea Bread

Prep Time: 15 minutes, Cook Time: 1 hour 35 minutes (plus cooling and standing), Serves:12

INGREDIENTS:

TEA BREAD

1½ tablespoons decaffeinated Earl Grey tea leaves

200 g granulated sugar   185 g plain flour

¼ teaspoon baking soda   ¼ teaspoon salt

115 g butter, softened

3 large eggs, at room temperature

1 teaspoon vanilla extract   120 g sour cream

LEMON GLAZE

80 g icing sugar

1 teaspoon freshly grated lemon peel

DIRECTIONS:

1. Preheat oven to 160°C. Grease 23 x 13-cm loaf pan and then dust with flour.

2. Prepare Tea Bread: In food processor with knife blade attached, finely grind tea leaves and granulated sugar. In medium bowl with wire whisk, mix flour, baking soda, and salt.

3. In large bowl with mixer on medium-high speed, beat butter and tea sugar until fluffy. Add eggs, 1 at a time. Beat in vanilla. Reduce speed to low. Alternately, add flour mixture and sour cream, beginning and ending with flour mixture, just until blended, occasionally scraping down sides of bowl with rubber spatula.

4. Spread batter in prepared loaf pan. Bake for 1 hour 20 minutes or until toothpick inserted in center of bread comes out clean. Cool bread in pan on wire rack for 10 minutes. Remove bread from pan; cool completely on wire rack.

5. Prepare Lemon Glaze: In small bowl with wire whisk, mix icing sugar, lemon peel, and 1 tablespoon water until smooth. Drizzle over bread; let stand until glaze is set. Bread can be made ahead, wrapped tightly in plastic wrap, and stored at room temperature for up to 4 days.

Mini Triple Chocolate Muffins

Prep Time: 20 minutes, Cook Time: 12 minutes, Serves:24 mini muffins

INGREDIENTS:

Butter, for greasing the pan (optional)

Flour, for dusting the pan (optional)

155 g plain flour   100 g brown sugar

40 g unsweetened cocoa powder

½ teaspoon table salt

½ teaspoon baking powder   ½ teaspoon baking soda

180 ml milk   80 ml vegetable or rapeseed oil

2 large eggs, at room temperature

2 teaspoons vanilla extract

40 g finely chopped semisweet chocolate

40 g finely chopped white chocolate

TOOLS/EQUIPMENT:

Mini muffin pan   Paper liners (optional)

2 medium bowls   Wire rack

DIRECTIONS:

1. Preheat the oven to 190°C.

2. Grease and lightly flour a 24-cup mini muffin pan or line with paper liners.

3. In a medium bowl, stir together the flour, brown sugar, cocoa powder, salt, baking powder, and baking soda.

4. In another bowl, stir together the milk, oil, eggs, and vanilla until well blended.

5. Make a well in the middle of the dry ingredients, then pour the wet ingredients in the middle and stir to mix. When almost blended, add the semisweet and white chocolate, and mix until just combined. Some small lumps are okay.

6. Spoon the batter into the muffin cups about ⅔ full. Bake for 8 to 12 minutes, or until a toothpick inserted into the middle of a muffin comes out clean. Cool slightly, then transfer the muffins to a wire rack to cool.

Quick Garlic Bread

Prep Time: 5 minutes, Cook Time: 8 minutes, Serves:4

INGREDIENTS:

230 g butter, at room temperature

2 garlic cloves, finely grated

2 tablespoons finely chopped fresh parsley

Freshly ground black pepper

1 baguette or ciabatta loaf

Flake salt, such as Maldon

TOOLS / EQUIPMENT

Fine grater   Small bowl

Bread knife   Aluminum foil

Baking sheet

DIRECTIONS:

1. Preheat the oven to 190°C.

2. In a small bowl, mix together the butter, garlic, and parsley, and season with pepper.

3. Using a bread knife, cut the baguette on the diagonal into 5 cm segments without slicing all the way through. Use a butter knife to spread all slices, both sides, with the butter mixture, and sprinkle with salt. Cut the baguette in half, and wrap each half in aluminum foil.

4. Lay the foil parcels on a baking sheet. Using a tea towel, remove one parcel after 5 minutes and give it a gentle squeeze. If it is warm to the touch and feels firm from developing a crust, then it is ready. If the bread is still soft and has more give, put the parcel back in the oven for 2 to 3 more minutes.

5. Open the foil parcels and allow to cool for a few minutes. Serve warm alongside a hearty dish of pasta, like Pasta with Homemade Tomato Sauce

Old-Fashioned White Sandwich Bread

Prep Time: 30 minutes (plus 1½ hours for dough to rise), Cook Time: 40 minutes, Serves:2 loaves (serves 24)

INGREDIENTS:

FOR THE BREAD

480 ml warm milk   2 tablespoons granulated sugar

1 (5 g) envelope active dry yeast

2 tablespoons butter, at room temperature

625 – 750 g plain all-flour   2 teaspoons table salt

1 tablespoon vegetable or rapeseed oil

Butter, for greasing the pans

FOR THE TOPPING

2 tablespoons butter, melted

TOOLS/EQUIPMENT:

Stand mixer or large bowl	Large bowl
Plastic wrap	2 loaf pans
Pastry brush	Wire rack

DIRECTIONS:

1. In the bowl of a stand mixer with the hook attachment on, stir together the warm milk, sugar, and yeast, then let it sit for about 5 minutes.
2. Add the 2 tablespoons room-temperature butter, 600 g of flour, and salt to the yeast mixture. Mix on low with the hook attachment until well blended. Add more flour as needed, a little at a time, until a dough forms. Raise the speed to medium, and continue kneading for 4 to 6 minutes, or until the dough is smooth and elastic.
3. Grease a large bowl with oil. Add the dough, turn it to coat, cover with plastic wrap and place in a warm, dark, draft-free place to double in size, about 1 hour. Punch down the dough, form it into 2 loaves, and place each in a greased loaf pan. Lightly brush the tops of the loaves with the melted butter. Cover with plastic wrap, and place in a warm, dark, draft-free place to rise again, about 30 minutes.
4. Preheat the oven to 175˚C.
5. Bake for 30 to 40 minutes or until browned and hollow-sounding when lightly tapped. Cool slightly, then remove and place on a wire rack to finish cooling.

PB&J Muffins

Prep Time: 35 minutes, Cook Time: 1 hr (plus cooling), Serves:12

INGREDIENTS:

FOR THE MUFFINS

6 tablespoons unsalted butter, cut into pieces	
80 g whole wheat flour	80 g plain flour
1 tablespoon baking powder	½ teaspoon salt
85 g creamy peanut butter	240 ml whole milk

100 g packed light brown sugar

1 teaspoon pure vanilla extract   2 large eggs

FOR THE TOPPINGS

170 g creamy peanut butter

110 g honey-roasted peanuts

320 g strawberry jam

DIRECTIONS:

1. Make the muffins: Preheat the oven to 175°. Line a 12-cup muffin pan with paper liners.
2. Microwave the butter in a small microwave-safe bowl until melted. Add the whole-wheat flour, plain flour, baking powder and salt to a large bowl and whisk to combine. Combine the melted butter, peanut butter, milk, brown sugar, vanilla and eggs in a medium bowl and whisk until smooth. Add the peanut butter mixture to the flour mixture and stir with a rubber spatula until just combined.
3. Pour the batter into the muffin cups with a small ladle or measuring cup, filling them three-quarters of the way. Tap the bottom of the pan lightly against the counter to smooth out the batter. Carefully place in the oven and bake until the muffins are lightly browned and a toothpick inserted into the centers comes out clean, about 25 minutes. Remove the pan from the oven with oven mitts and place it on a wire rack to cool for 5 minutes. Remove the muffins from the pan and place on the rack to cool completely.
4. Make the toppings: Using a teaspoon, scoop out a shallow hole in the middle of each muffin. Microwave the peanut butter in a small microwave-safe bowl, stirring with a spoon halfway through, until loose, 45 to 60 seconds.
5. Finely chop the peanuts with a chef's knife and spread on a plate. Dip the top of a muffin in the melted peanut butter, letting the excess drip off, then dip it in the chopped peanuts to coat. Place on the rack and repeat with the remaining muffins.
6. Spoon 1 heaping tablespoon jelly or jam into the hole in each muffin. Let set 5 minutes.

Spiced Plum & Quinoa Muffins

Prep Time: 20 minutes, Cook Time: 35 minutes, Serves:18 muffins

INGREDIENTS:

155 g plain flour

125 g whole wheat flour

55 g white quinoa, uncooked

1½ teaspoons baking powder

1 teaspoon ground cinnamon

½ teaspoon ground ginger

½ teaspoon baking soda

½ teaspoon salt

2 large eggs, beaten

240 g plain full-fat yogurt

115 g butter, melted

185 g honey

3 plums, 1 chopped and 2 thinly sliced

DIRECTIONS:

1. Preheat oven to 200°C. Line eighteen muffin-pan cups with paper liners. In a large bowl with wire whisk, mix flours, quinoa, baking powder, cinnamon, ginger, baking soda, and salt.

2. In medium bowl with wire whisk, beat eggs, yogurt, melted butter, and honey until blended. Fold egg mixture into flour mixture just until blended; stir in chopped plums. Divide batter among prepared muffin-pan cups and top each with a couple of plum slices.

3. Bake for 15 to 20 minutes or until toothpick inserted into centers of muffins comes out clean. Cool muffins in pans for 5 minutes. Remove muffins from pans and cool completely on wire racks.

S'mores Muffins

Prep Time: 25 minutes, Cook Time: 1 hour (plus cooling), Serves:12

INGREDIENTS:

170 g milk chocolate chips

125 g plain flour

230 g unsalted butter, cut into pieces

15 digestive biscuits, broken into crumbs

2 teaspoons baking powder

½ teaspoon salt

150 g sugar

120 ml whole milk

1 teaspoon pure vanilla extract

2 large eggs

180 g marshmallow cream

DIRECTIONS:

1. Preheat the oven to 175°. Line a 12-cup muffin pan with paper liners. Toss the chocolate chips with 2 teaspoons flour in a small bowl; set aside.

2. Microwave the butter in a separate small microwave-safe bowl until melted. Add the remaining flour, the biscuit crumbs, baking powder and salt to a large bowl and whisk to combine. Combine the melted butter, sugar, milk, vanilla and eggs in a medium bowl and whisk until smooth. Add the butter mixture to the flour mixture and stir with a rubber spatula until just combined. Add the chocolate chip mixture and stir with the spatula.

3. Pour the batter into the muffin cups with a small ladle or measuring cup, filling them three-quarters of the way. Tap the bottom of the pan lightly against the counter to smooth out the batter. Carefully place in the oven and bake until the muffins are lightly browned and a toothpick inserted into the centers comes out clean, 20 to 25 minutes. Remove the pan from the oven with oven mitts and place on it a wire rack to cool for 5 minutes. Remove the muffins from the pan and place on the rack to cool completely.

4. Spoon 1 tablespoon marshmallow cream onto each muffin. Let set 10 minutes.

Yogurt Banana Bread

Prep Time: 20 minutes, Cook Time: 60 minutes, Serves:1 loaf (serves 12)

INGREDIENTS:

Butter, for greasing the pan

Flour, for dusting the pan

200 g plan flour

1 teaspoon baking soda

½ teaspoon cinnamon

½ teaspoon table salt

2 large eggs, at room temperature

175 g granulated sugar

340 g mashed, very ripe bananas (3 to 5 bananas)

120 ml vegetable or rapeseed oil

2 tablespoons plain Greek yogurt

1 teaspoon vanilla extract

TOOLS/EQUIPMENT:

Loaf pan   2 medium bowls

DIRECTIONS:

1. Preheat the oven to 175°C.

2. Lightly grease and flour a loaf pan.

3. In a medium bowl, mix together the flour, baking soda, cinnamon, and salt until well combined.

4. In another medium bowl, beat together the eggs and sugar for 3 to 5 minutes, or until light and fluffy. Stir in the banana, oil, yogurt, and vanilla until just combined.

5. Make a well in the center of the dry ingredients. Pour the wet ingredients into the well. Stir until just combined.

6. Pour the batter into the prepared loaf pan. Bake at 175°C for 45 to 60 minutes, or until a toothpick inserted in the center comes out clean.

Corn Muffins

Prep Time: 10 minutes, Cook Time: 55 minutes (plus cooling time), Serves:12 muffins

INGREDIENTS:

Vegetable oil spray   190 g plain flour

125 g polenta   1½ teaspoons baking powder

1 teaspoon baking soda ½ teaspoon salt

100 g sugar   2 large eggs

180 g sour cream   8 tablespoons unsalted butter

melted and cooled   120 ml whole milk

TOOLS/EQUIPMENT:

12-cup muffin tin   2 bowls (1 large, 1 medium)

Whisk   Rubber spatula

¼-cup dry measuring cup   Toothpick

Oven mitts   Cooling rack

DIRECTIONS:

1. Adjust oven rack to middle position and heat oven to 190 degrees. Spray 12-cup muffin tin, including top, with vegetable oil spray.

2. In medium bowl, whisk together flour, polenta, baking powder, baking soda, and salt.

3. In large bowl, whisk sugar and eggs until well combined, light-coloured, and thick, about 1 minute. Add sour cream, melted butter, and milk and whisk to combine.

4. Add flour mixture and use rubber spatula to gently stir until just combined and no dry flour is visible. Do not overmix.

5. Spray ¼-cup dry measuring cup with vegetable oil spray. Use greased measuring cup to divide batter evenly among muffin cups.

6. Place muffin tin in oven. Bake until muffins are golden brown and toothpick inserted into center of 1 muffin comes out clean for 20 to 25 minutes.

7. Use oven mitts to remove muffin tin from oven (ask an adult for help). Place muffin tin on cooling rack and let muffins cool in muffin tin for 15 minutes.

8. Using your fingertips, gently wiggle muffins to loosen from muffin tin and transfer directly to cooling rack. Let muffins cool for at least 10 minutes before serving.

Tender Chocolate Chip Mini Muffins

Prep Time: 10 minutes, Cook Time: 45 minutes, plus 20 minutes cooling time, Serves:24 mini muffins

INGREDIENTS:

Vegetable oil spray   165 g plain flour
½ teaspoon baking soda   ¼ teaspoon salt
2 very ripe bananas (skins should be speckled black)
100 g sugar   4 tablespoons unsalted butter, melted and cooled   60 g plain yogurt
1 large egg   ½ teaspoon vanilla extract
50 g) mini chocolate chips

TOOLS/EQUIPMENT:

Gather Baking Equipment   24-cup mini muffin tin
2 bowls (1 large, 1 medium)   Whisk
Large fork or potato masher   Rubber spatula
1-tablespoon measuring spoon   Toothpick
Oven mitts   Cooling rack

DIRECTIONS:

1. Adjust oven rack to middle position and heat oven to 190 degrees. Spray 24-cup mini muffin tin well with vegetable oil spray (make sure to get inside each mini cup!).
2. In medium bowl, whisk together flour, baking soda, and salt.
3. Peel bananas and place in large bowl. Use large fork or potato masher to mash bananas until broken down but still chunky.
4. Add sugar, melted butter, yogurt, egg, and vanilla to bowl with bananas and whisk until combined.
5. Add flour mixture and chocolate chips and use rubber spatula to gently stir until just combined and no dry flour is visible. Batter should look thick and chunky—do not overmix.
6. Spray 1-tablespoon measuring spoon with vegetable oil spray. Use greased measuring spoon to scoop 1 heaping tablespoon batter into each muffin tin cup.
7. Place muffin tin in oven. Bake until muffins are golden brown and toothpick inserted in center of 1 muffin comes out clean, 13 to 15 minutes.
8. Use oven mitts to remove muffin tin from oven. Place muffin tin on cooling rack and let muffins cool in muffin tin for 15 minutes.
9. Using your fingertips, gently wiggle muffins to loosen from muffin tin and transfer directly to cooling rack. Let muffins cool for at least 5 minutes before serving.

Whole-Wheat Raspberry Muffins

Prep Time: 10 minutes, Cook Time: 55 minutes, plus 25 minutes cooling time, Serves:12 muffins

INGREDIENTS:

Vegetable oil spray   405 g whole-wheat flour
2½ teaspoons baking powder
½ teaspoon baking soda
1 teaspoon salt   2 large eggs
4 tablespoons unsalted butter melted and cooled
60 ml vegetable oil   175 g sugar
2 tablespoons sugar, measured separately
300 ml buttermilk   1½ teaspoons vanilla extract
250 g fresh or frozen raspberries (do not thaw if frozen)

TOOLS/EQUIPMENT:

12-cup muffin tin   2 bowls (1 large, 1 medium)
Whisk   Rubber spatula
Dry measuring cup   Toothpick
Oven mitts   Cooling rack

DIRECTIONS:

1. Adjust oven rack to middle position and heat oven to 190 degrees. Spray 12-cup muffin tin, including top, with vegetable oil spray.
2. In medium bowl, whisk together flour, baking powder, baking soda, and salt.
3. In large bowl, whisk eggs, melted butter, oil, and 200 g sugar until combined. Add buttermilk and vanilla to sugar mixture and whisk until well combined.
4. Add flour mixture and use rubber spatula to gently stir until just combined and no dry flour is visible. Gently stir raspberries into batter. Do not overmix.
5. Spray dry measuring cup with vegetable oil spray. Use greased measuring cup to divide batter evenly among muffin cups. Sprinkle remaining 2 tablespoons sugar evenly over batter.
6. Place muffin tin in oven. Bake until muffins are golden brown and toothpick inserted in center of 1 muffin comes out clean, 20 to 25 minutes.
7. Use oven mitts to remove muffin tin from oven (ask an adult for help). Place muffin tin on cooling rack and let muffins cool in muffin tin for 15 minutes.
8. Using your fingertips, gently wiggle muffins to loosen from muffin tin and transfer directly to cooling rack. Let muffins cool for at least 10 minutes before serving.

Basic Muffins

Prep Time: 15 MINUTES, Cook Time: 35 MINUTES, Serves:12 MUFFINS

INGREDIENTS:

310 g plain flour   100 g sugar   240 ml milk   6 tablespoons butter, melted

1 tablespoon baking powder   ½ teaspoon salt   1 teaspoon vanilla extract   1 large egg

DIRECTIONS:

1. Preheat oven to 200°C. Grease twelve muffin-pan cups. In large bowl with wire whisk, mix flour, sugar, baking powder, and salt. In small bowl with fork, beat milk, melted butter, vanilla, and egg until well blended. Add liquid mixture to flour mixture; stir just until flour is evenly moistened. Spoon batter into prepared muffin-pan cups.

2. Bake for 18 to 20 minutes or until toothpick inserted in centers of muffins comes out clean. Immediately remove muffins from pan. Serve warm, or cool on wire rack.

Chapter 4: Cookies & Bars

Chocolate Pecan Tassie Cookie Cups

Prep Time: 30 minutes, Cook Time: 30 minutes, Serves:24 cookies

INGREDIENTS:

FOR THE COOKIES

115 g unsalted butter, at room temperature

75 g plain cream cheese, at room temperature

125 g plain flour

FOR THE FILLING

1 large egg   150 g brown sugar

1 tablespoon unsalted butter, melted

35 g chopped pecans   55 g mini chocolate chips

TOOLS/EQUIPMENT:

2 medium bowls   Electric mixer

Mini muffin pan (24-cup)   Wire rack

DIRECTIONS:

1. Preheat the oven to 160˚C.
2. In a medium bowl, beat together 115 g of room-temperature butter and the cream cheese with an electric mixer on medium speed until well blended. Beat in the flour until just blended.
3. In another medium bowl, whisk together the egg, brown sugar, and melted butter until well blended. Stir in the pecans and chocolate chips.
4. Press a rounded teaspoon of cookie dough in each cup of an ungreased 24-cup mini muffin pan. Press the dough in the middle so it goes up the sides to form a little cookie cup. Spoon the filling into each cookie cup about ¾ full.
5. Bake for 25 to 30 minutes, or until golden brown and slightly puffed. Cool slightly in the pan, then transfer the cookies to a wire rack to finish cooling.

Crispy Meringue Cookies

Prep Time: 10 minutes, Cook Time: 1 hour and 30 minutes, plus drying and cooling, Serves:12 cookies

INGREDIENTS:

3 large eggs, cold   ½ teaspoon cream of tartar

200 g granulated white sugar

1 teaspoon vanilla extract

20 g cocoa powder (optional)

TOOLS/EQUIPMENT:

Measuring cups and spoons   Sheet pan

Parchment paper

Mixing bowl, plus 2 small bowls for separating the eggs

Electric hand mixer   Oven-safe gloves

Sifter or fine-mesh sieve

DIRECTIONS:

1. Preheat your oven to 110°C. Line a sheet pan with parchment paper.
2. Separate the egg whites from the yolks, placing the whites in a super clean mixing bowl.
3. Add the cream of tartar to the egg whites. Using an electric hand mixer, mix on low speed. Once you get some foam, raise the speed to medium. Once the mixture turns white, raise the speed to high.
4. Add the sugar 1 tablespoon at a time so the egg whites can get big, fluffy, and glossy. If you see any sugar grains, keep mixing! You want your egg white mixture to be smooth.
5. Once the mixture is fluffy, add the vanilla. Continue whisking until fully mixed.
6. Turn off the mixer. Take 1 heaping tablespoon of your meringue, and spoon onto the prepared baking sheet. Repeat with the remaining meringue, leaving room in between.
7. Put the sheet pan in the oven. Bake for 1 hour. Don't peek!
8. Turn off the oven. Leave the sheet pan inside for 1 hour to completely dry the meringues. Keep the oven door closed as it could deflate and crack them.
9. Using oven-safe gloves, remove the sheet pan from the oven. Let cool for 45 minutes.
10. Dust the meringues with the cocoa powder (if using).

Classic Lemon Bars

Prep Time: 30 minutes (plus 2 hours chill time),

Cook Time: 50 minutes, Serves:16 bars

INGREDIENTS:

FOR THE CRUST

125 g plain flour

180 g unsalted butter, at room temperature

30 g icing sugar

Butter, for greasing the pan

⅛ teaspoon table salt

2 tablespoons brown sugar

FOR THE FILLING

2 large eggs, at room temperature   1 large egg yolk

200 g granulated sugar 3 tablespoons plain flour

½ teaspoon freshly grated lemon zest

120 ml freshly squeezed lemon juice (3 or 4 lemons)

FOR THE GARNISH

2 tablespoons icing sugar

TOOLS/EQUIPMENT:

20 cm square baking pan

Large bowl

Whisk or fork

Small bowl

Electric mixer

Zester

DIRECTIONS:

1. Preheat the oven to 175°C.
2. Lightly grease an 20 cm square baking pan.
3. In a small bowl, stir together 125 g of flour and the salt.
4. In a large bowl, beat the butter with an electric mixer on medium speed for about 10 seconds, or until smooth. Beat in 30 g of icing sugar and the brown sugar until well blended and light and fluffy, about 2 minutes. Add the flour mixture to the butter mixture until just combined. Press the dough evenly onto the bottom of the pan and about 1 cm up the sides of the pan to form the crust.
5. Bake for 15 to 20 minutes, or until golden brown around the edges.
6. Meanwhile, in a large bowl whisk together the eggs, egg yolk, granulated sugar, 3 tablespoons of flour, lemon zest, and lemon juice until well blended.
7. Remove the crust from the oven and reduce the oven temperature to 150°C. Pour the filling over the cooked crust. Bake for 25 to 30 minutes, or until the filling appears set (firm). Cool the bars, then refrigerate for at least 2 to 3 hours, or until firm enough to cut into bars. Dust with 2 tablespoons of icing sugar before serving.

Crispy Chocolate Chip Cookies

Prep Time: 10 minutes, Cook Time: 40 minutes plus cooling, Serves:24 cookies

INGREDIENTS:

230 g unsalted butter, softened

205 g packed dark brown sugar

200 g granulated white sugar

1 ½ tablespoons heavy cream

2 eggs, at room temperature   ½ teaspoon salt

1 ½ teaspoons vanilla extract   375 g plain flour

¾ teaspoon baking soda   ½ teaspoon baking powder

335 g semisweet chocolate chips

TOOLS/EQUIPMENT:

Measuring cups and spoons

Parchment paper

Mixing bowl

Oven-safe gloves

Wire rack

Sheet pan

Electric hand mixer

Ice-cream scoop

Offset spatula

DIRECTIONS:

1. Preheat your oven to 190°C. Line a sheet pan with parchment paper.
2. Using an electric hand mixer in a mixing bowl, cream together the butter, brown sugar, and granulated white sugar for 2 minutes on high speed.
3. Add the cream, eggs, salt, and vanilla. Mix until combined and glossy.
4. Add the flour, baking soda, and baking powder. Mix until there are no visible dry spots.
5. Reduce the mixer speed to low, and fold in the chocolate chips.
6. Using an ice-cream scoop, scoop about 12 dough balls onto the sheet pan. Give them some room because they will expand and flatten.
7. Put the sheet pan in the oven. Bake for 10 to 12 minutes, or until the edges of the cookies are golden brown and they look delicious.
8. Using oven-safe gloves, remove the sheet pan from the oven. Transfer the cookies using an offset spatula to a wire rack to cool for about 10 minutes.
9. Repeat with the remaining dough or keep it in an airtight container in the refrigerator for up to 3 days or in the freezer for up to 3 months.

Double Chocolate Chip Cookies

Prep Time: 20 minutes, Cook Time: 40 minutes (plus cooling), Serves:2 dozen cookies

INGREDIENTS:

185 g plain flour   180 g packed brown sugar   ½ teaspoon baking soda   ¼ teaspoon salt
115 g butter, softened (no substitutions)   1 large egg   125 g semisweet chocolate chips
50 g granulated sugar   125 g white chocolate chips
2½ teaspoons vanilla extract

DIRECTIONS:

1. Preheat oven to 190°C.
2. In large bowl with mixer on medium speed, beat all ingredients except semisweet and white chocolate chips until blended and smooth, occasionally scraping bowl with rubber spatula. With spoon, stir in chips.
3. Drop dough by rounded tablespoonfuls onto large ungreased cookie sheet, 5 cm apart. Bake for 10 to 12 minutes or until golden. With metal spatula, immediately transfer cookies to wire rack to cool. Repeat with remaining dough. Cookies can be made ahead and stored in an airtight container at room temperature for up to 1 week.

Frosted Sugar Cookie Pops

Prep Time: 45 minutes (plus 2 hours chill time), Cook Time: 14 minutes, Serves:24 cookie pops

INGREDIENTS:

FOR THE COOKIES

375 g plain flour   ¾ teaspoon baking powder
¼ teaspoon table salt
230 g unsalted butter, at room temperature
200 g granulated sugar   1 large egg
1 tablespoon milk   1 teaspoon vanilla extract
Butter, for greasing the baking sheets (optional)

FOR THE FROSTING

115 g) unsalted butter, at room temperature
500 g icing sugar   ½ teaspoon vanilla extract
3 to 6 tablespoons whole milk
Food colouring (optional)   Sprinkles (optional)

TOOLS/EQUIPMENT:

Medium bowl   Large bowl
Electric mixer   Plastic wrap
2 baking sheets   Parchment paper (optional)
Rolling pin   Round cookie cutter
White lollipop sticks   Wire rack

DIRECTIONS:

1. In a medium bowl, stir together the flour, baking powder, and salt.
2. In a large bowl, beat 230 g of butter with an electric mixer on medium speed for about 10 seconds or until smooth. Beat in the granulated sugar until well blended and light and fluffy, about 2 minutes. Beat the egg, 1 tablespoon of milk, and 1 teaspoon of vanilla until well blended.
3. Add the flour mixture to the butter and sugar mixture, and beat with an electric mixer on medium speed until blended.
4. Divide the dough in half, and place each half on a large piece of plastic wrap. Flatten each piece to form a large disk, then wrap tightly with plastic wrap. Refrigerate for at least 2 hours or until firm.
5. Preheat the oven to 190°C.
6. Lightly grease 2 baking sheets or line with parchment paper.
7. Roll out one piece of dough on a lightly floured surface to ½ cm thick. Using a 8 cm round cookie cutter, cut out circles. Place the circles on the prepared baking sheets. Gently press a lollipop stick about 1 cm into each cookie from the side. Use cookie dough scraps to cover the stick if it pops through.
8. Bake for 9 to 14 minutes, or until golden brown around the edges, rotating the pans halfway through baking. Cool slightly, then transfer the cookies to a wire rack to finish cooling.
9. In a medium bowl, beat 115 g of butter with an electric mixer for about 10 seconds or until smooth. Gradually beat in the icing sugar and ½ teaspoon vanilla. Add 2 tablespoons of milk and beat until smooth, adding a little more milk, one tablespoon at a time, as needed. Add a few drops of food colouring, if desired. Once cookies are completely cooled, frost them and decorate with sprinkles, if desired.

Honey Roasted Peanut Butter Cookies

Prep Time: 20 minutes (plus 30 minutes chill time), Cook Time: 17 minutes, Serves:24 cookies

INGREDIENTS:

345 g plain flour   1¼ teaspoons baking soda

¼ teaspoon table salt

180 g unsalted butter, at room temperature

50 g shortening   255 g brown sugar

100 g plus 1 tablespoon granulated sugar, divided

255 g creamy peanut butter

2 large eggs, at room temperature

2 teaspoons vanilla extract

145 g chopped honey roasted peanuts

TOOLS/EQUIPMENT:

Medium bowl	Large bowl
Electric hand mixer	Plastic wrap
2 baking sheets	Parchment paper (optional)
Fork	Wire rack

DIRECTIONS:

1. In a large bowl, beat the butter and shortening with an electric mixer on medium speed for about 10 seconds, or until smooth. Beat in the brown sugar and 100 g of granulated sugar until well blended and light and fluffy, about 2 minutes. Beat in the peanut butter, then beat in the eggs one at a time, beating after each addition. Beat in the vanilla until well blended.
2. Beat the flour mixture into the butter and sugar mixture until just combined. With a spoon, stir in the nuts.
3. Cover the dough with plastic wrap and refrigerate for a half-hour or more, until firm.
4. Preheat the oven to 190˚C.
5. Drop the cookie dough in big (3-tablespoon) lumps onto ungreased baking sheets or baking sheets lined with parchment paper, leaving about 5 cm between cookies. Gently press down on the cookies with a fork (up and down, and side to side) to make a crisscross pattern. Sprinkle lightly with the remaining tablespoon of sugar. Bake for 13 to 17 minutes, or until golden brown around the edges, rotating the pans halfway through baking. Cool slightly, then transfer the cookies to a wire rack to cool completely.

Marble Cookies

Prep Time: 15 minutes, Cook Time: 10 minutes, Serves:6

INGREDIENTS:

220 g plain flour, divided   ¼ teaspoon salt

1 teaspoon baking soda   660 g butter, softened

175 g granulated sugar   175 g brown sugar

2 large eggs   1 teaspoon vanilla extract

6 tablespoons cocoa powder

175 g chocolate sprinkles

TOOLS/EQUIPMENT

Baking sheet   Parchment paper or silicone baking mat

2 medium bowls and 1 large bowl   Spatula

Cooling rack   Cookie scoop

Small metal spatula

DIRECTIONS:

1. Preheat the oven to 190°C, and line a baking sheet with parchment paper or a silicone baking mat.
2. In a medium bowl, combine flour, salt, and baking soda. Set aside.
3. In a large bowl, combine the butter, granulated sugar, and brown sugar, and mix until smooth. Add the eggs and vanilla, and mix until blended. Add the flour and baking soda mixture, and mix until smooth and creamy.
4. Divide the dough in half, placing one half into the medium bowl you used for the flour mixture and the other half in another medium bowl. Add the remaining 65 g of flour to one batch of dough, and the cocoa powder to the other batch. Mix both doughs until smooth and creamy. Scoop the light dough into balls about the size of a walnut and place on a piece of parchment paper. Repeat with the chocolate dough.
5. Take one of each colour ball of dough, press together and flatten so that one side is half light and the other is half dark. Roll the edges liberally in the chocolate sprinkles. Place on the baking sheet 2.5 cm apart, and bake for 11 minutes. Don't let the edges brown.
6. Let the cookies cool for a few minutes, and then, using a cookie spatula, transfer them to a cooling rack until completely cool. Store in an airtight container.

Mini "Black & White" Cookies

Prep Time: 30 MINUTES, Cook Time: 1 HOUR (PLUS COOLING AND STANDING) , Serves:3 DOZEN COOKIES

INGREDIENTS:

COOKIES

250 g plain flour	½ teaspoon baking soda
¼ teaspoon salt	180 g butter, softened
200 g granulated sugar	2 large eggs

120 ml low-fat buttermilk

ICING

400 g icing sugar	2 tablespoons light
corn syrup	
2 tablespoons milk	⅛ teaspoon salt
assorted food colourings	

DIRECTIONS:

1. Prepare Cookies: Arrange oven racks in top and bottom thirds of your oven. Preheat oven to 175°C. Line 2 large cookie sheets with parchment paper.

2. In medium bowl with wire whisk, mix flour, baking soda, and salt. In large bowl with mixer on medium speed, beat butter and granulated sugar for 3 minutes or until fluffy. Add eggs, 1 at a time. Reduce speed to low. Alternately add flour mixture and buttermilk, beginning and ending with flour mixture, just until blended. Drop dough by rounded tablespoonfuls on prepared cookie sheets, 5 cm apart.

3. Bake for 13 to 15 minutes or until golden, rotating cookie sheets between upper and lower racks halfway through baking. Transfer cookies to wire racks and cool completely.

4. Prepare Icing: In large bowl with mixer on low speed, beat icing sugar, corn syrup, milk, and salt until smooth. Tint half the icing in bowls with food colouring, as desired. Spread icing on cookies' flat sides. Let stand for 30 minutes or until set.

Oat Pear Bars

Prep Time: 30 minutes, Cook Time: 40 minutes, Serves:16 bars

INGREDIENTS:

Butter, for greasing the pan	90 g plain flour
60 g rolled oats	½ teaspoon baking powder
½ teaspoon table salt	
3 tablespoons unsalted butter, melted and cooled	
100 g brown sugar	1 large egg yolk
½ teaspoon vanilla extract	

320 g peeled, cored, and finely chopped pear (2 or 3 pears)

3 tablespoons maple syrup

TOOLS/EQUIPMENT:

20 cm square baking pan	Medium bowl
Large bowl	Electric mixer
Small saucepan	Slotted spoon

DIRECTIONS:

1. Preheat the oven to 175°C.

2. Lightly grease an 20 cm square baking pan.

3. In a medium bowl, stir together the flour, oats, baking powder, and salt.

4. In a large bowl, beat together the melted butter and brown sugar with an electric mixer on medium speed until well blended and light and fluffy, about 2 minutes. Beat in the egg yolk, then beat in the vanilla.

5. Beat the flour mixture into the butter and sugar mixture until just combined.

6. Spread about ⅔ of the cookie batter evenly over the bottom of the prepared pan. Using your fingers or the back of a fork, press down to make an even layer. Bake the crust for 10 to 15 minutes, or until slightly puffed and golden brown around the edges.

7. Meanwhile, in a small saucepan over medium heat, heat the chopped pears and maple syrup. Cook for 5 to 7 minutes, or until the pears begin to soften.

8. Remove the crust from the oven. With a slotted spoon, spoon the pears over the top of the crust. Sprinkle the remaining cookie batter on top. Bake for 15 to 20 minutes, or until the edges are slightly browned. Cool completely before cutting into bars.

Pb&J Bars

Prep Time: 30 minuteS, Cook Time: 1 hour 15 minutes (plus cooling) , Serves:24 bars

INGREDIENTS:

230 g softened (no substitutions)   200 g sugar   140 g salted, dry-roasted peanuts, coarsely chopped

130 g creamy peanut butter   1 large egg   320 g strawberry jam

375 g plain flour

DIRECTIONS:

1. Preheat oven to 175°C. Line 13 x 23 cm metal baking pan with foil; grease foil.

2. In large bowl with mixer on low speed, beat butter and sugar until mixed, occasionally scraping bowl with rubber spatula. Increase speed to high; beat until light and fluffy. Reduce speed to low; beat in peanut butter, then egg until well combined, occasionally scraping bowl. Beat in flour just until evenly moistened (dough will be crumbly). Beat in peanuts.

3. Reserve 2 cups dough. Press remaining dough into prepared baking pan into even layer. Spread jam over dough in pan. With your hands, break the reserved 2 cups of dough into large chunks (about 1.5 cm pieces). Drop chunks over jam, leaving spaces between clumps of dough; do not pat down.

4. Bake for 45 to 50 minutes or until golden. Cool bars completely, in pan, on wire rack.

5. When cool, using foil, transfer bars to cutting board. Cut bars lengthwise into 3 strips, then cut each strip crosswise into 8 pieces.

Raspberry-Rhubarb Crumb Bars

Prep Time: 30 minutes, Cook Time: 1 hour 25 minutes (plus cooling) , Serves:16 bars

INGREDIENTS:

220 g plain flour   175 g packed light brown   245 g raspberries   175 g granulated sugar

sugar   2 tablespoons cornflour

½ teaspoon baking soda   ½ teaspoon salt   2 tablespoons fresh orange juice

180 g cold butter, cut up 45 g sliced almonds   2 teaspoons vanilla extract

250 g sliced rhubarb stems, sliced 1 cm thick

DIRECTIONS:

1. Preheat oven to 175°C. Line 8 x 20 cm metal baking pan with parchment paper, extending 5 cm over rim.

2. In food processor with knife blade attached, pulse flour, brown sugar, baking soda, and salt until combined. Add butter and pulse just until dough resembles coarse crumbs. Press ⬚ of dough into bottom of prepared baking pan. Bake 15 minutes or until pale golden; place on a wire rack to cool until warm but not hot.

3. Stir almonds into remaining crumb mixture; press to form large crumbs.

4. In large bowl, combine rhubarb, raspberries, granulated sugar, cornflour, orange juice, and vanilla; spread over warm crust. Sprinkle with crumb topping.

5. Bake 40 to 45 minutes or until filling is bubbling. Cool bars completely, in pan, on wire rack. When cool, using parchment, transfer bars to cutting board. Cut into 16 squares.

Rosemary Shortbread Cookies

Prep Time: 20 minutes, plus 40 minutes to chill, Cook Time: 15 minutes, Serves:2 dozen cookies

INGREDIENTS:

220 g plain flour

20 g flax meal

1 tablespoon finely chopped fresh rosemary

¾ teaspoon sea salt

460 g unsalted butter, at room temperature

50 g icing sugar, sifted

TOOLS / EQUIPMENT

Medium sieve for sifting

Electric mixer

Baking sheets

Parchment paper

2 large bowls

Rubber spatula

Wire cooling rack

DIRECTIONS:

1. In a large bowl, mix the flour, flax meal, rosemary, and salt until well combined. Set aside.
2. In another large bowl, use an electric mixer to cream the butter, about 4 minutes. Add the sugar and blend until fluffy, scraping down the sides with a spatula.
3. Add the flour mixture to the butter mixture, and blend on low, just until a dough forms. Test by squeezing the dough between your fingers—if it holds together, it's ready. Working quickly, roughly squeeze dough into a cylindrical shape. Wrap the parchment over it and roll dough back and forth into an even, solid roll, about 30 cm long. The ends should be the same thickness as the center.
4. Refrigerate the dough log for 20 minutes.
5. Preheat the oven to 175°C.
6. Remove the dough from the refrigerator, and unwrap the parchment paper. Use a sharp knife to cut the dough into ½ cm-thick disks. Arrange them on baking sheets and refrigerate until firm, about 20 minutes. Bake for 15 minutes, or until the edges and bottoms are golden.
7. Transfer the cookies onto a wire cooling rack to cool fully. Cookies will keep for 4 days between layers of parchment, sealed, at room temperature.

Spiced Oatmeal Raisin Cookies

Prep Time: 20 minutes (plus 2 hours chill time), Cook Time: 17 minutes, Serves:12 cookies

INGREDIENTS:

100 g old-fashioned rolled oats   90 g plain flour

¾ teaspoon cinnamon   ½ teaspoon table salt

½ teaspoon baking powder

⅛ teaspoon ground cloves

⅛ teaspoon ground nutmeg

⅛ teaspoon ground ginger

115 g unsalted butter, at room temperature

175 g granulated sugar   2 tablespoons molasses

1 large egg   1 teaspoon vanilla extract

145 g raisins

TOOLS/EQUIPMENT:

Medium bowl   Large bowl

Electric mixer   Plastic wrap

Baking sheets   Parchment paper (optional)

Wire rack

DIRECTIONS:

1. In a medium bowl, stir together the oats, flour, cinnamon, salt, baking powder, cloves, nutmeg, and ginger.
2. In a large bowl, beat the butter with an electric mixer on medium speed for about 10 seconds or until smooth. Beat in the sugar and molasses until well blended and light and fluffy, about 2 minutes. Beat in the egg, then beat in vanilla until well blended.
3. Add the flour mixture to the butter and sugar mixture, and beat with an electric mixer on medium speed until blended. With a spoon, stir in the raisins.
4. Cover the dough with plastic wrap and refrigerate for at least 2 hours or overnight to firm up.
5. Preheat the oven to 175°C.
6. Bake the cookies.
7. Drop the cookie dough in big (3-tablespoon) lumps onto ungreased baking sheets or baking sheets lined with parchment paper, leaving about 5 cm between cookies. Bake for 13 to 17 minutes, or until golden brown around the edges, rotating the pans halfway through cooking. Cool slightly, then transfer the cookies to a wire rack to cool completely.

Swap-It-Your-Way Sweet & Salty Cookies

Prep Time: 15 minutes, Cook Time: 35 minutes (plus cooling), Serves:2 dozen cookies

INGREDIENTS:

415 g plain flour	40 g cornflour	300 g packed brown sugar	175 g granulated sugar
1½ teaspoons baking powder		2 large eggs	1 tablespoon vanilla extract
1¼ teaspoons baking soda		40 g grated courgette	110 g chopped peanuts
1½ teaspoons salt	290 g butter, softened	30 g broken pretzels	

DIRECTIONS:

1. Arrange oven racks in the top and bottom thirds of the oven. Preheat oven to 175°C. In a medium bowl with a wire whisk, mix flour, cornflour, baking powder, baking soda, and salt.

2. In a large bowl with mixer on medium speed, beat butter and sugars until light and fluffy. Beat in the eggs, 1 at a time. Beat in vanilla, then flour mixture just until blended. Fold in Veggie Scraps and Chunks.

3. Scoop dough by scant (or just barely full) onto 2 large ungreased cookie sheets, about 2.5 cm apart. Bake for 20 to 25 minutes, or until bottoms are golden brown, rotating cookie sheets between upper and lower racks halfway through baking. Cool cookies completely, on cookie sheets, on wire racks.

Thick And Chewy Chocolate Chip Cookies

Prep Time: 30 minutes (plus 2 hours chill time), Cook Time: 18 minutes, Serves:30 cookies

INGREDIENTS:

415 g plain flour	1 tablespoon cornflour
1 teaspoon baking powder	1 teaspoon baking soda
1 teaspoon table salt	
230 g unsalted butter, melted and cooled slightly	
200 g brown sugar	200 g granulated sugar
1 large egg	2 large egg yolks

1 teaspoon vanilla extract 300 g bag mini chocolate chips

TOOLS/EQUIPMENT:

Medium bowl	Large bowl
Electric hand mixer	Plastic wrap
2 baking sheets	Parchment paper (optional)
Wire rack	

DIRECTIONS:

1. In a medium bowl, stir together the flour, cornflour, baking powder, baking soda, and salt.

2. In a large bowl, beat the melted butter, brown sugar, and granulated sugar with an electric mixer on medium speed until well blended and light and fluffy, about 2 minutes. Beat in the egg and egg yolks, then beat in vanilla until well blended.

3. Add the flour mixture to the butter and sugar mixture, and beat with an electric mixer on medium speed until blended. With a spoon, stir in the chocolate chips.

4. Drop the dough in large (3-tablespoon) lumps on a large baking sheet or 2 baking sheets, leaving about 5 cm between cookies. Cover the dough with plastic wrap and refrigerate at least 2 hours or overnight.

5. Preheat the oven to 160°C.

6. Bake for 15 to 18 minutes on ungreased baking sheets or baking sheets lined with parchment paper, or until lightly browned around the edges, rotating the pans halfway through cooking. Cool slightly, then transfer the cookies to a wire rack to cool completely.

Strawberry Cheesecake Bars

Prep Time: 15 minutes (plus 3 hours chill time), Cook Time: 40 minutes, Serves:16 bars

INGREDIENTS:

FOR THE CRUST

Butter, for greasing the pan

10 to 12 digestive biscuits

4 tablespoons unsalted butter, melted

FOR THE CHEESECAKE

2 (200 g) bricks cream cheese, at room temperature

100 g granulated sugar

2 large eggs, at room temperature

½ teaspoon vanilla extract

FOR THE STRAWBERRY SAUCE

455 g frozen strawberries, thawed   50 g granulated sugar

1 teaspoon vanilla extract

TOOLS/EQUIPMENT:

20 cm square baking pan	2 medium bowls
Electric mixer	Blender

DIRECTIONS:

1. Preheat the oven to 175˚C.
2. Lightly grease an 20 cm square baking pan.
3. In a medium bowl, mix together the digestive biscuit crumbs and melted butter. Press the mixture evenly into the bottom of the pan.
4. In another medium bowl, beat the cream cheese with an electric mixer on medium speed until smooth. Beat in 100 g of sugar until well blended. Beat in the eggs one at a time, beating after each addition, then beat in ½ teaspoon of vanilla. Pour the mixture over the crust.
5. Bake for 30 to 40 minutes, or until center is almost set (firm). Let cool, then refrigerate at least 3 hours, or overnight, until fully chilled.
6. Meanwhile, in a blender, add the thawed strawberries, 50 g of granulated sugar, and 1 teaspoon of vanilla. Pulse repeatedly until smooth.
7. Once the cheesecake is fully chilled, cut it into bars, and drizzle with a little strawberry sauce before serving.

Chapter 5: Pizza

Breakfast Pizza

Prep Time: 15 minutes, Cook Time: 15 minutes, Serves:4

INGREDIENTS:

Olive oil   Salt

Freshly ground black pepper

15 asparagus spears, woody ends trimmed

10 slices ham, torn into pieces

100 g shredded Monterey Jack cheese

60 g shredded mozzarella

4 large eggs, each cracked into a separate small bowl or ramekin

TOOLS/EQUIPMENT

Grater   4 small bowls or ramekins

Pizza stone or baking sheet

Basting brush (or paper towel)   Large bowl

Pizza cutter or knife   Flour, for dusting the pan

1 disk fresh pizza dough, store-bought or from a pizza shop

DIRECTIONS:

1. Position an oven rack in the middle of the oven. Prepare a pizza stone or baking sheet by scattering flour lightly onto the surface. Preheat the oven to 230°C.

2. Shape the pizza dough into either a rustic rectangle or a traditional round, depending on the shape of your pan. Brush the dough lightly with oil, and season with salt and pepper.

3. Place a small amount of oil in your clean hands. In a large bowl, toss the asparagus spears with your hands, lightly coating them. Season the asparagus with salt and pepper, then arrange the asparagus in a sunburst pattern, with the tips pointing outward.

4. Place in the oven and bake for 5 minutes. Remove from the oven, place ham all over the pizza, top with the cheeses, and slide each egg onto a separate quarter of the pizza. Sprinkle the eggs with salt and pepper, and quickly return the pizza to the oven. Bake for an additional 10 minutes, or until the crust is golden and the eggs are set to your liking. Cool slightly, slice into 4 wedges, and serve.

Classic Margherita Pizza

Prep Time: 15 minutes, Cook Time: 30 minutes, Serves:4

INGREDIENTS:

180 g marinara sauce

150 g fresh mozzarella cheese, thinly sliced

25 g grated Parmesan cheese

5 g packed fresh basil, sliced

DIRECTIONS:

1. Place large cookie sheet in oven. Preheat oven to 245°C.

2. Stretch dough into small circle. Place dough on large sheet of parchment paper, stretching and pressing to form 36 cm circle with slight rim. Spread sauce on dough; top evenly with mozzarella. Remove hot cookie sheet from oven. Carefully slide parchment with dough onto hot cookie sheet (ask an adult if you need help).

3. Sprinkle pizza with Parmesan. Place pizza in oven; bake for 15 to 20 minutes or until bottom is crisp and golden brown. Top with basil.

Mini Mexican Pizzas

Prep Time: 30 minutes, Cook Time: 37 minutes, Serves:12 pizzas

INGREDIENTS:

Olive oil, for greasing the baking sheets

1 prepared Homemade Pizza Dough

Flour, for dusting the work surface   200 g beef mince

2 tablespoons taco seasoning

180 ml plain tomato sauce

200 g shredded Cheddar cheese

30 g shredded lettuce   110 g finely chopped tomato

110 g guacamole   15 g crushed tortilla chips

TOOLS/EQUIPMENT:

2 baking sheets   Rolling pin

Large frying pan

DIRECTIONS:

1. Preheat the oven to 190˚C.
2. Lightly grease 2 baking sheets with olive oil.
3. Divide the pizza dough into 12 balls. On a lightly floured surface, roll out each dough ball into thin circles, 10 – 13 cm wide. Place on the baking sheets.
4. Bake for 10 to 15 minutes, or until just light golden brown.
5. Meanwhile, in a large frying pan over medium-high heat, heat the beef mince. Cook, stirring occasionally while breaking up the beef, 5 to 7 minutes, or until thoroughly browned. Drain the grease. Add the taco seasoning to the beef, and stir to combine.
6. Spoon the tomato sauce on top of each pizza crust, leaving about a 1 cm border around the edges. Sprinkle the cheese over the sauce, then spoon the ground beef on top.
7. Bake for 10 to 15 minutes, or until the dough is golden brown and cheese is bubbly.
8. Top each pizza with the lettuce and tomato. Place a dollop of the guacamole on each pizza and sprinkle with the crushed chips.

Personal Margherita Pizzas

Prep Time: 10 minutes, Cook Time: 40 minutes, Serves:6 PIZZAS

INGREDIENTS:

1 tablespoon olive oil, plus more for greasing the pan

1 recipe Pizza Dough

Plain flour, for rolling the dough

700 g canned San Marzano tomatoes, crushed

1 teaspoon salt   1 teaspoon granulated white sugar

1 teaspoon dried oregano

120 g torn fresh mozzarella cheese

15 g fresh basil leaves

TOOLS/EQUIPMENT:

Measuring cups and spoons   Can opener

Sheet pan   Knife

Rolling pin   Mixing bowl

Wooden spoon   Plastic wrap

Oven-safe gloves

DIRECTIONS:

1. Preheat your oven to 230°C. Grease a sheet pan with olive oil.
2. Cut the dough into 6 portions. Lightly flour a clean work surface and rolling pin. Roll out the dough, and place on the prepared sheet pan.
3. To make the pizza sauce, in a mixing bowl, stir together the tomatoes, oil, salt, granulated white sugar, and oregano.
4. Spread the tomato sauce onto the dough.
5. Top each pizza with the cheese and basil.
6. Put the sheet pan in the oven. Bake for 5 to 7 minutes, or until the cheese is melted and the crust is golden brown.
7. Using oven-safe gloves, remove the sheet pan from the oven.

Pizza Primavera

Prep Time: 15 minutes, Cook Time: 40 minutes, Serves:4

INGREDIENTS:

1 bunch asparagus, trimmed and thinly sliced on an angle

½ small red onion, very thinly sliced

2 tablespoons olive oil

½ teaspoon ground black pepper

Pizza-Tastic Dough

100 g shredded mozzarella cheese

DIRECTIONS:

1. Place large cookie sheet in oven. Preheat oven to 245°C. Meanwhile, in large bowl, combine asparagus, onion, oil, and pepper, tossing to coat.
2. Stretch dough round into small circle. Place dough on large sheet of parchment paper, stretching to form 15 cm circle with slight rim. Sprinkle fontina evenly on dough. Then sprinkle asparagus mixture on top of cheese.
3. Remove hot cookie sheet from oven. Carefully slide parchment with dough onto hot cookie sheet (ask an adult if you need help). Place pizza in oven; bake for 20 to 25 minutes or until bottom and edges are deep golden brown.

Pizza-Tastic Dough

Prep Time: 15 minutes, Cook Time: 10 minutes (plus chilling and standing), Serves:455 g dough

INGREDIENTS:

375 g plain flour

1 teaspoon instant yeast

1 tablespoon sugar

1 tablespoon plus 2 teaspoons olive oil

1 teaspoon salt

DIRECTIONS:

1. In food processor with knife blade attached, pulse flour, sugar, and yeast. With machine running, drizzle in 240 ml plus 2 tablespoons warm water until combined. Add 1 tablespoon olive oil and salt. Process until dough forms a ball; transfer to lightly oiled large bowl.
2. With lightly oiled hands, knead dough for 1 minute. Form into ball; drizzle with remaining 2 teaspoons olive oil, rubbing to coat surface. Cover dough tightly with plastic wrap and refrigerate for at least 1 day or for up to 3 days. Let stand at room temperature for 1 hour before using.

Spicy Sausage & Cheese Pizza

Prep Time: 10 minutes, Cook Time: 30 minutes, Serves:4

INGREDIENTS:

1 teaspoon olive oil

1 large (30 cm) store-bought, prebaked thin pizza crust

120 ml marinara sauce

70 g finely chopped fully cooked chorizo sausage

100 g shredded mozzarella cheese

75 g roasted red peppers, thinly sliced

½ small red onion, thinly sliced

3 tablespoons finely chopped fresh parsley, for garnish

DIRECTIONS:

1. Preheat oven to 220°C. Brush large cookie sheet with oil. Place crust on prepared cookie sheet.
2. Spread marinara sauce on crust in even layer. Top evenly with sausage, cheese, roasted peppers, and onion.
3. Bake for 15 to 20 minutes or until crust is golden brown and cheese has melted. Garnish with parsley.

Spinach-Artichoke Pizza

Prep Time: 10 minutes, Cook Time: 25 minutes, Serves:4

INGREDIENTS:

1 loaf soft French or Italian bread   2 tablespoons olive oil
150 g shredded mozzarella cheese
250 g frozen chopped spinach, thawed and squeezed dry
200 g reduced-fat cream cheese, softened
80 g fat-free Greek yogurt or light sour cream

35 g grated Parmesan cheese
2 garlic cloves, crushed in press ¼ teaspoon salt
¼ teaspoon ground black pepper
225 g frozen artichokes, thawed, patted dry, and chopped
1 lemon   snipped fresh chives, for garnish

DIRECTIONS:

1. Preheat oven to 200°C. Line large cookie sheet with foil. Cut bread in half lengthwise, then cut each piece in half across. With your hands, press bread to flatten.

2. Arrange bread, cut sides up, on prepared cookie sheet. Brush with oil and sprinkle with 120 g mozzarella. Bake for 5 to 7 minutes or until cheese melts.

3. In large bowl, mix spinach, cream cheese, yogurt, Parmesan, garlic, salt, and pepper until blended. Remove bread from oven and divide cheese mixture among pieces of bread, spreading evenly. Top with artichokes and remaining mozzarella. Bake for 12 to 18 minutes longer or until golden brown.

4. Grate peel of half the lemon over pizzas. Garnish with chives.

Thin-Crust Veggie Pizza

Prep Time: 10 minutes, Cook Time: 25 minutes, Serves:4

INGREDIENTS:

nonstick cooking spray   4 (20 cm) flour tortillas
120 g baby spinach
1 medium red pepper, very thinly sliced
1 medium courgette, very thinly sliced
2 teaspoons minced garlic   2 teaspoons olive oil

½ teaspoon salt   ½ teaspoon ground black pepper
180 ml marinara sauce   100 goat cheese, crumbled
25 g finely grated Parmesan cheese
5 g fresh basil leaves

DIRECTIONS:

1. Arrange oven racks in top and bottom thirds of oven. Preheat oven to 245°C. Spray 2 large cookie sheets with nonstick cooking spray; place 2 tortillas on each.

2. In large microwave-safe bowl, combine spinach, red pepper, courgette, garlic, oil, salt, and black pepper; tossing to coat. Microwave uncovered on high for 2 minutes or until crisp-tender, stirring once. Drain, if necessary. Spread marinara sauce on tortillas. Top with vegetables and cheeses.

3. Bake for 12 minutes or until tortillas are crisp around edges, switching racks halfway through baking. When baked, take out of oven and top with basil.

Chapter 6: Fruit Desserts

Banana-Berry Split

Prep Time: 10 minutes, Cook Time: 0, Serves:4

INGREDIENTS:

4 bananas   150 g vanilla yogurt, divided

85 g chocolate chips or chocolate shavings

150 g blueberries or your favourite berry

Chocolate sauce or caramel sauce, for drizzling

Multicoloured sprinkles, for garnish

TOOLS/EQUIPMENT

Cutting board   Knife

4 serving bowls

DIRECTIONS:

1. Peel the bananas and halve them lengthwise. In each of 4 bowls, position 2 banana halves side by side, spoon 120 g of the yogurt over top of each, and sprinkle each with the chocolate chips and berries.
2. Drizzle with chocolate and/or caramel sauce, dust with colourful sprinkles, and serve.

Flognarde (Apple-Custard Bake)

Prep Time: 15 minutes, Cook Time: 30 minutes, Serves:4

INGREDIENTS:

4 tablespoons butter, cubed, plus more for greasing the pan

5 tablespoons flour   4 tablespoons sugar

Zest of 2 lemons   160 ml whole milk

4 eggs 3 apples, peeled, cored, and cut into 1 cm

wedges

Icing sugar, for dusting

TOOLS / EQUIPMENT

Zester   Vegetable peeler

Large cast-iron   frying pan

Medium bowl   Whisk

DIRECTIONS:

1. Preheat the oven to 200°C.
2. In a medium bowl, mix together the flour, sugar, lemon zest, and milk. Add the eggs and beat vigorously. Continue whisking as you pour the mixture into the pan.
3. Fan the apple wedges and lay them onto the mixture. It's okay if they slide a little as you arrange them.
4. Dot the surface with butter, and bake until the custard puffs and has turned golden brown at the edges, about 30 minutes.
5. Dust icing sugar onto the custard. Serve hot or at room temperature, cut into wedges.

Cheesecake-Stuffed Strawberries

Prep Time: 25 minutes, Cook Time: 0, Serves:6

INGREDIENTS:

455 g fresh strawberries, rinsed and patted dry

200 g block cream cheese, softened

60 g icing sugar   1 teaspoon vanilla extract

TOOLS/EQUIPMENT

Paper towel	Cutting board
Paring knife	Stand or hand mixer
Spatula	Piping bag with tip or plastic baggie

DIRECTIONS:

1. Using a paring knife, remove the stems from the strawberries. Cut a small piece off the bottom tip of each berry so the berry will stand on its own. Core the strawberries by cutting a circular opening into the berry, making a small hollow.

2. With a mixer, mix the cream cheese, icing sugar, and vanilla until smooth, creamy, and fluffy, about 2 minutes.

3. Gently pat the berry openings with a paper towel. Spoon the cream cheese mixture into a piping bag or plastic baggie with a corner snipped off. Stuff the berries with the cream cheese mixture. Serve or refrigerate until ready to serve.

Homemade Apple Crisp

Prep Time: 10 minutes, Cook Time: 1 hour and 10 minutes, plus 30 minutes cooling ti, Serves:

INGREDIENTS:

80 g plain flour   40 g oats

50 g packed light brown sugar

½ teaspoon ground cinnamon

5 tablespoons unsalted butter, melted and cooled

50 g sugar   2 teaspoons cornflour

⅛ teaspoon salt

900 g Golden Delicious apples, peeled, cored, and cut into 2.5 cm pieces

TOOLS/EQUIPMENT:

2 bowls (1 large, 1 medium)	Rubber spatula
Fork	20 cm square baking dish
Oven mitts	Cooling rack

DIRECTIONS:

1. Toss oat mixture with fork or your fingers until mixture comes together. Adjust oven rack to lower-middle position and heat oven to 190 degrees.

2. In medium bowl, use rubber spatula to stir together flour, oats, brown sugar, and cinnamon. Drizzle melted butter over oat mixture and toss with fork or your fingers until mixture comes together (see photo, below).

3. In large bowl, use rubber spatula to stir together sugar, cornflour, and salt. Add apples to bowl with cornflour mixture and toss to coat.

4. Use rubber spatula to scrape apple mixture into 20 cm square baking dish. Crumble oat topping into pea-size clumps and sprinkle oat topping evenly over apple mixture.

5. Place baking dish in oven. Bake until filling is bubbling around edges and topping is golden brown, about 40 minutes.

6. Use oven mitts to remove baking dish from oven (ask an adult for help). Place baking dish on cooling rack and let apple crisp cool on rack for at least 30 minutes before serving.

Lemon Soufflés

Prep Time: 20 minutes, Cook Time: 20 minutes, Serves:6

INGREDIENTS:

2 tablespoons butter, softened

5 tablespoons granulated sugar, divided

3 large egg yolks, plus 5 large egg whites

240 ml milk

1 tablespoon vanilla extract   30 g plan flour

4 tablespoons freshly squeezed lemon juice, plus 2 tablespoons lemon zest, finely grated

1 tablespoon icing sugar, plus more for dusting

TOOLS/EQUIPMENT

Microplane or zester	6 (200 g) ramekins
Baking sheet	3 small bowls
Heavy saucepan	Medium bowl
Whisk	Knife
Mesh strainer	

DIRECTIONS:

1. Preheat the oven to 200°C.

2. Using your fingertips, coat 6 ramekins with the butter. Dust the ramekins with 2 tablespoons of granulated sugar, rolling it around the sides and emptying the excess out into the next ramekin. Place the ramekins on a baking sheet in the refrigerator to chill.

3. Separate the eggs, placing the yolks in one small bowl and egg whites in another. Chill the egg whites until ready to use.

4. In a heavy saucepan, bring the milk to a boil. Remove from the heat.

5. In a medium bowl, whisk together the egg yolks, vanilla, and 1 tablespoon of granulated sugar. Whisk in the flour. Whisk 60 ml of the hot milk into the egg yolk mixture until blended. Continue mixing the hot milk into the egg yolk mixture, 60 ml at a time, until all the milk is incorporated.

6. Pour the mixture back into the saucepan, and stir constantly over medium-low heat until thickened, about 2 minutes, moving the pot on and off the heat as you do so the mixture does not get too hot. If clumps begin to form, remove from the heat and whisk vigorously to smooth it out (see Troubleshooting). Remove the custard from the heat.

7. In a small bowl, mix together the lemon zest, lemon juice, and icing sugar, and then add to the custard, whisking until smooth.

8. Beat the egg whites on high speed until they hold soft peaks. Sprinkle the remaining 2 tablespoons of granulated sugar over the egg whites, and beat until stiff and shiny. Fold ¼ of the egg whites into the custard until the whites disappear. Fold in the remaining egg whites until just blended; don't over blend or you'll deflate the egg whites and the batter will turn soupy.

9. Spoon the batter into the ramekins, filling just to the top. Level the tops with a knife. Use your finger to go around the inside perimeter of each ramekin to clean the edges.

10. Reduce the oven temperature to 190°C, and immediately place the ramekins in the oven on a baking sheet. Bake until puffed and the tops turn golden brown, 12 to 14 minutes. They should still be wobbly; move them slowly and carefully.

11. Use a small mesh strainer to sprinkle with icing sugar and enjoy immediately.

Peach-Blueberry Crisp

Prep Time: 10 minutes, Cook Time: 45 minutes, Serves:4

INGREDIENTS:

50 g oats

65 g packed brown sugar, plus 3 tablespoons for fruit

30 g plus 2 tablespoons plain flour, divided

½ teaspoon ground cinnamon

2 teaspoons fresh ginger, finely grated Salt

180 g butter, freezer-cold and cubed

900 g peaches or nectarines, cut into thin wedges

295 g blueberries

2 teaspoons freshly squeezed lemon juice

1 teaspoon lemon zest

TOOLS / EQUIPMENT

Zester	Citrus reamer
2 large bowls	Ceramic or glass
baking dish	Baking sheet
Wire cooling rack	

DIRECTIONS:

1. In a large bowl, stir with a fork to combine the oats, 65 g of brown sugar, 30 g plus 1 tablespoon of flour, and the cinnamon. Add the ginger, a pinch of salt, and the butter to the mixture, and work the butter into the dry ingredients with your fingers until pea-size crumbs remain. Refrigerate.

2. Preheat the oven to 190°C.

3. In another large bowl, stir together the peaches and blueberries with the lemon juice and zest, the remaining 3 tablespoons of brown sugar, the remaining tablespoon of flour, and a pinch of salt. Toss all to combine.

4. Pour the fruit mixture into a baking dish, then spoon the oat mixture on top to coat. On a baking sheet, bake the crisp until the topping is golden and the juices bubble, 30 to 45 minutes. Allow the crisp to cool on a wire cooling rack for at least 20 minutes.

5. The crisp is delicious served warm, room temp, or even cold. It's so virtuous you could even eat it for breakfast! This fruity number is excellent all by itself, but it would be amazing topped with ice cream.

Roasted Strawberry Parfait

Prep Time: 15 minutes, Cook Time: 15 minutes, Serves:4

INGREDIENTS:

305 g fresh strawberries, hulled and quartered

1½ tablespoons brown sugar

240 g mascarpone cheese

240 g plain Greek yogurt   2 tablespoons honey

½ tablespoon freshly squeezed lemon juice

TOOLS/EQUIPMENT

Cutting board	Paring knife
Baking sheet	Parchment paper or silicone baking mat
Large bowl	Mixer
4 small glasses	

DIRECTIONS:

1. Preheat the oven to 220°C. Line a baking sheet with parchment paper or a silicone baking mat.

2. In a large bowl, toss the berries with the brown sugar. Spread the berries evenly on the prepared baking sheet, and roast for 10 to 15 minutes, just until the berries begin to release their juices.

3. Meanwhile, use a mixer to whip the mascarpone cheese for 1 minute on high. Add the yogurt, honey, and lemon juice, and mix until just combined.

4. Into each of 4 small glasses, spoon a layer of yogurt. Top with the berries. Repeat the layers, ending with berries on top, and serve.

Sautéed Apples

Prep Time: 10 minutes, Cook Time: 25 minutes, Serves:4 TO 6

INGREDIENTS:

2½ tablespoons butter

6 firm, tart apples, such as Granny Smith or Honeycrisp, peeled and cut into small cubes

175 g brown sugar

60 g chopped walnuts or raisins (or both)

1½ teaspoons ground cinnamon

½ teaspoon ground nutmeg   Pinch salt

TOOLS/EQUIPMENT

Cutting board   Knife

Large sauté pan   Wooden spoon

Small mason jars or serving bowls

DIRECTIONS:

1. In a large sauté pan over medium-low heat, melt the butter. Add the apples and brown sugar and sauté, stirring often, for 15 minutes, or until the apples are soft.

2. Add the walnuts and/or raisins, cinnamon, nutmeg, and salt. Stir to mix well, and sauté for an additional 6 to 8 minutes, or until thickened.

3. Remove from the heat, spoon into small mason jars or serving bowls, and serve.

Strawberry Granita

Prep Time: 10 minutes, plus about 1 hour 30 minutes to freeze, Cook Time: 0, Serves:4

INGREDIENTS:

455 g cleaned and hulled strawberries

1 teaspoon lemon zest   240 ml hot water

100 g sugar

2 tablespoons freshly squeezed lemon juice

TOOLS/EQUIPMENT

Cutting board   Paring knife

Microplane or zester

Food processor or high-powered blender

Medium bowl   13-by-23 cm pan or metal bowl

Fork   Small glasses or bowls

DIRECTIONS:

1. In a food processor or high-powered blender, purée the berries until smooth. Mix in the zest and set aside.

2. In a medium bowl, combine the hot water, sugar, and lemon juice, and stir until the sugar is dissolved. Add the strawberry mixture to the sugar mixture, and stir to combine.

3. Pour the mixture into a 13-by-23 cm pan or a metal bowl, and place in the freezer for 30 minutes. Remove from the freezer (edges should be icy), and stir up the granita with a fork, moving the icy parts to the center of the bowl as you do. Return the granita to the freezer, and repeat the process two more times (30 minutes apart each time). Once the granita is dry and frozen, scrape with a fork into small glasses or bowls and serve immediately.

Watermelon-Lime Sorbet

Prep Time: 10 minutes, plus 6 hours to freeze, Cook Time: 1 minute, Serves:6

INGREDIENTS:

900 g cubed watermelon   60 ml water

3 tablespoons sugar

60 ml freshly squeezed lime juice (2 to 3 limes)

TOOLS/EQUIPMENT

Baking sheet   Parchment paper or wax paper

Small pot

Food processor or high-powered blender

DIRECTIONS:

1. Line a baking sheet with parchment paper or wax paper. Spread the watermelon cubes on the baking sheet, and freeze for 30 minutes. Transfer the cubes to a freezer-safe container in the freezer for at least 6 hours or overnight.

2. When ready to make the sorbet, make a simple syrup by heating the water and sugar in a small pot over medium heat and stirring. Once the sugar is dissolved, remove from the heat. Place the frozen watermelon and lime juice in a food processor or high-powered blender, drizzle in the warm simple syrup, and blend until the watermelon breaks down into an icy slush. Enjoy immediately or freeze for 30 minutes.

Apple Stuffing

Prep Time: 20 minutes, Cook Time: 4–5 hours, Serves:4 to 5

INGREDIENTS:

115 g butter, divided   120 g chopped walnuts   applesauce

2 onions, chopped   water, optional

350 g pkg. dry herb-seasoned stuffing mix 365 g

DIRECTIONS:

1. In nonstick frying pan, melt 2 Tbsp. of butter. Sauté walnuts over medium heat until toasted, about 5 minutes, stirring frequently. Remove from frying pan and set aside.

2. Melt remaining butter in frying pan. Add onions and cook 3–4 minutes, or until almost tender. Set aside.

3. Spray slow cooker with nonstick cooking spray. Place dry stuffing mix in slow cooker.

4. Add onion-butter mixture and stir. Add applesauce and stir.

5. Cover and cook on Low 4–5 hours, or until heated through. Check after Stuffing has cooked for 3½ hours. If it's sticking to the cooker, drying out, or becoming too brown on the edges, stir in 120 – 240 ml water. Continue cooking.

6. Sprinkle with walnuts before serving.

Chapter 7: Salad

Asian Noodle Salad

Prep Time: 15 minutes, Cook Time: 10 minutes, Serves:8 TO 10

INGREDIENTS:

FOR THE SAUCE

120 ml soy sauce   3 tablespoons sesame oil

2 tablespoons red wine vinegar or rice wine vinegar

2 tablespoons olive oil

1 tablespoon plus 1 teaspoon sugar

1½ tablespoons chili sauce with garlic

FOR THE SALAD

455 g linguine

1 red pepper, sliced thin into 2.5 – 5 cm long pieces

4 or 5 spring onions, sliced thin

TOOLS/EQUIPMENT

Cutting board	Knife
Glass jar with lid	Large pot
Wooden spoon	Strainer or colander
Paper towels	Tongs (optional)
Serving bowl	

DIRECTIONS:

1. In a jar with a lid, combine all the sauce ingredients. Cover and shake vigorously to mix well.
2. In a large pot, cook the pasta according to package directions for for al dente (firm).
3. Drain the noodles, then run under cold water until cool. Shake as much water out as you can, then blot the noodles dry with paper towels. Dry the pot, return the noodles to the pot, and pour half the sauce over them. Toss with tongs or clean hands to coat every noodle.
4. Add in most of the peppers and spring onions, and toss to mix. Transfer to a serving bowl. Arrange the rest of the peppers and spring onions on top, and pour the remaining sauce over top. Cover and let stand at room temperature until ready to serve.

Chicken Salad Wraps

Prep Time: 15 minutes, Cook Time: 0, Serves:4

INGREDIENTS:

Heaping 60 g coarsely chopped carrots

1½ stalks celery, cut into 2.5 cm chunks

675 g chicken meat, from a rotisserie chicken or cooked chicken breasts   120 g – 180 g mayonnaise

Salt   Freshly ground black pepper

4 flour tortilla wraps   Lettuce, for serving

TOOLS/EQUIPMENT

Cutting board	Knife
Food processor	Rubber spatula
Large bowl	

DIRECTIONS:

1. In a food processor, pulse the carrots and celery until minced. Chop or tear the chicken into 2.5 cm chunks, add to the food processor, and pulse a few times until chopped. Add the mayonnaise, salt and pepper to taste, and pulse until combined. Taste and adjust if needed. Scrape the chicken salad into a large bowl.
2. Place a couple leaves of lettuce onto each wrap, add a dollop of chicken salad, roll up burrito-style, and serve.

Colourful Crunch Salad

Prep Time: 15 minutes, Cook Time: 5 minutes, Serves:4

INGREDIENTS:

4 red, orange, and yellow bell peppers, cored and sliced into thin, bite-size strips

2 celery stalks, diced

1 handful green beans, ends trimmed, sliced into thin coins

5 g chopped fresh parsley

2 tablespoons capers, rinsed and chopped

2 tablespoons olive oil

2 teaspoons sherry or champagne vinegar

Freshly ground black pepper   30 g slivered almonds

TOOLS / EQUIPMENT

Toaster oven

DIRECTIONS:

1. Arrange almonds in a single layer on a toaster oven tray. Toast for 4 minutes, or until they become fragrant and their edges turn golden. You may agitate pan halfway through, circulating the almonds for even toasting. Transfer them to a small dish.

2. Layer the peppers, celery, green beans, parsley, and capers onto a serving platter. Toss slightly to incorporate.

3. Drizzle the salad with the olive oil and vinegar, season with pepper, and scatter the toasted almonds on top. Serve immediately.

Easy Cobb Salad

Prep Time: 15 minutes, Cook Time: 0, Serves:4

INGREDIENTS:

1 head iceberg lettuce or 2 romaine hearts, stems removed, torn into bite-size pieces

230 g chopped grape tomatoes

120 g cooked crumbled bacon

2 avocados, peeled, pitted, and sliced

3 large hard-boiled eggs, chopped

Homemade Ranch Dressing or favourite dressing, for serving

TOOLS/EQUIPMENT

Cutting board   Chef's knife

Large bowl or 4 small bowls

DIRECTIONS:

1. Put the lettuce in 1 large salad bowl or divide evenly among 4 individual bowls. Top with the ingredients, giving each their own "row" next to one another atop the lettuce: a row of tomatoes, a row of bacon, a row of avocados, and a row of eggs.

2. Serve immediately, along with Homemade Ranch Dressing or your favourite dressing.

Egg Salad And Toast Points

Prep Time: 10 minutes, Cook Time: 15 minutes, Serves:4

INGREDIENTS:

8 eggs   Ice water

4 slices crusty bread, such as sourdough or seeded wheat, crusts removed, and cut diagonally in half, into triangles

2 tablespoons mayonnaise

2 teaspoons Dijon mustard

1 teaspoon freshly squeezed lemon juice

1 celery stalk, finely chopped

1 tablespoon finely chopped cornichons

1 tablespoon finely chopped parsley   Sea salt

Freshly ground black pepper

TOOLS / EQUIPMENT

Citrus reamer   Large saucepan

Large bowl   Large

slotted spoon   Toaster oven

Medium bowl

DIRECTIONS:

1. In a saucepan large enough for the eggs to sit in a single layer, bring to a boil enough water to submerge the eggs by at least 2.5 cm. Carefully lower the eggs into the water, return to a boil, and simmer for 10 minutes. Have a large bowl filled with ice water nearby.

2. Use a slotted spoon to transfer the eggs to the water to chill them for peeling. Let the eggs sit in the ice bath until cool to the touch. Tap the eggshell on your work surface, turning it and cracking it throughout. Peel the shells and discard.

3. Toast the bread pieces in the toaster oven until golden and crisp. Transfer to individual plates or a serving dish.

4. In a medium bowl, use a fork or potato masher to mash the hard-cooked eggs, combining them with the mayonnaise, mustard, and lemon juice. You may opt to keep the consistency chunky, or for a creamier consistency, mash until well combined.

5. Add the celery, cornichons, and parsley, and season with salt and pepper. Stir gently to combine.

6. Serve with the toast points chilled or at room temperature. Any leftovers will keep, sealed in the refrigerator, for up to 4 days.

Grainy Mustard-Potato Salad

Prep Time: 10 minutes, Cook Time: 10 minutes, Serves:4

INGREDIENTS:

6 medium Yukon gold potatoes, scrubbed and cut into chunky wedges

3 medium red potatoes, scrubbed and cut into chunky wedges

4 to 5 tablespoons olive oil

2 tablespoons whole-grain mustard

1 tablespoon capers, well-rinsed and chopped

1 shallot, sliced thin

3 tablespoons dill, torn into small sprigs Sea salt

Freshly ground black pepper

TOOLS / EQUIPMENT

Large saucepan   Colander

Large bowl

DIRECTIONS:

1. In a large saucepan, cover the potatoes with water and gently boil them for 8 to 10 minutes, until fork-tender. Drain the potatoes in a colander, and transfer to a large bowl.

2. In a large bowl, toss the olive oil, mustard, capers, and shallot to combine with the potatoes.

3. Once the potato mixture has cooled to room temperature, add the dill sprigs, and toss again. Season to taste with salt and pepper. Enjoy warm, at room temperature, or chilled.

Honey-Lime Fruit Salad

Prep Time: 15 minutes, Cook Time: 0, Serves:4

INGREDIENTS:

150 g strawberries, halved   150 g blueberries

150 g grapes, halved   Zest of ½ lime

2 tablespoons freshly squeezed lime juice

2 tablespoons honey (more to taste if you want it sweeter)

TOOLS/EQUIPMENT

Cutting board   Knife

Microplane or zester   Serving bowl

DIRECTIONS:

1. In a serving bowl, toss together the strawberries, blueberries, and grapes.
2. Sprinkle the lime zest onto the fruit, toss with the lime juice, and serve.

Nutty Parmesan-Kale Salad

Prep Time: 15 minutes, Cook Time: 10 minutes, Serves:4

INGREDIENTS:

1 bunch Lacinato kale, also known as Tuscan or dinosaur kale, rinsed, ends trimmed

Zest and juice of 1 lemon   2 tablespoons olive oil

Flake salt, such as Maldon

Freshly ground black pepper

115 g hazelnuts   50 g shaved Parmigiano-Reggiano

TOOLS / EQUIPMENT

Citrus reamer   Zester

Vegetable peeler   Large bowl

Baking sheet   Toaster oven

Small serving bowl

DIRECTIONS:

1. Gather the kale into a tight bunch or stack the leaves on top of each other, and slice into very thin strips, about ¼ cm wide. Transfer to a large bowl.

2. Add the lemon zest and juice and the olive oil to the bowl, season with salt and pepper, and toss to combine. Taste and adjust seasoning, and set aside.

3. Toast the hazelnuts for 5 minutes or until fragrant. When cool enough to handle, gently rub off their skins. Arrange the nuts on a cutting board. Coarsely crush them by leaning your weight onto the side of a chef's knife placed on them. Transfer nuts to the toaster oven tray and toast again until golden, about 3 minutes more. Empty the nuts into a small serving bowl.

4. At the table, scatter the hazelnuts and shaved Parm over the salad, and serve immediately.

Orzo Pesto Salad

Prep Time: 10 minutes, Cook Time: 10 minutes, Serves:6

INGREDIENTS:

225 g orzo pasta

1 tablespoon olive or grapeseed oil

1 bunch asparagus   Salt

150 g halved grape tomatoes   4 spring onions, sliced thin

Freshly ground black pepper

4 to 5 tablespoons pesto, store-bought or homemade

TOOLS/EQUIPMENT

Cutting board   Knife

Large pot   Colander

Large bowl   Small pot

Mixing spoon

DIRECTIONS:

1. In a large pot, cook the orzo according to package directions for al dente (firm). Strain the pasta in a colander, and immediately begin running cold water over it to completely cool it down. Drain it well. Transfer to a large bowl, toss with the oil, and set aside.

2. Slice the tips off the asparagus, then cut another 2.5 cm piece off of each spear, reserving the rest of the asparagus for another use. Fill a small pot halfway with water, salt the water (about 1 tablespoon), and bring to a boil. Add the asparagus pieces and blanch for 1 to 2 minutes, until crisp-tender. Drain the asparagus tips in a colander, and immediately run under cold water to stop the cooking process.

3. Add the asparagus, tomatoes, and spring onions to the bowl with the orzo. Season with salt and pepper, and toss to mix. Add the pesto, toss again to coat, and serve.

Shaved Brussels Sprouts Salad

Prep Time: 20 minutes, Cook Time: 0, Serves:4

INGREDIENTS:

455 g Brussels sprouts, woody stems removed, grated or shredded

1 large sweet apple, such as Honeycrisp, or tart apple, such as Granny Smith, chopped or cut into thin half-moons

30 g pumpkin seeds, pistachios, or walnut pieces

Lemon Vinaigrette

75 g or more freshly shaved Parmesan cheese

TOOLS/EQUIPMENT

Cutting board   Knife

Grater   Medium bowl

Wooden spoon   Salad tongs

DIRECTIONS:

1. In a medium bowl, combine the Brussels sprouts, apples, and pepitas. Toss to combine. Add 3 tablespoons of Lemon Vinaigrette, tossing to coat.

2. Use tongs to transfer the salad to individual serving plates. Sprinkle each plate with shaved Parmesan, and serve with extra dressing on the side.

Chapter 8: Sandwich, Brownies & Tarts

Blackened Tuna Sandwiches

Prep Time: 10 minutes, plus 15 minutes to sit, Cook Time: 5 minutes, Serves:2

INGREDIENTS:

60 g mayonnaise   Handful fresh basil, chopped

2 (150 g) fresh tuna steaks

3 tablespoons blackening seasoning

2 to 3 tablespoons olive or grapeseed oil

2 round rolls   Lettuce leaves

Sliced tomato

TOOLS/EQUIPMENT

Cutting board   Knife

Small bowl   Large nonstick frying pan or sauté pan

Metal spatula

DIRECTIONS:

1. Let the tuna sit at room temperature for 15 minutes. Meanwhile, in a small bowl, mix the mayonnaise and basil. Set aside.

2. Generously coat the tuna in the blackening seasoning. In a large, nonstick sauté pan or frying pan over medium-high heat, heat the oil. Once very hot, add the tuna steaks and cook for 3 minutes on each side for medium. Add additional oil to the pan if the pan looks dry.

3. Slice open the rolls horizontally, and spread the cut sides of the rolls with the basil mayonnaise. Place some lettuce and a tomato slice on the bottom half of each roll. Top each with a cooked tuna steak and serve.

Cheesy Egg Sandwich

Prep Time: 5 minutes, Cook Time: 10 minutes, Serves:4

INGREDIENTS:

Olive oil, for drizzling and frying

1 baguette or other crusty bread, sliced into 13 cm sections and halved horizontally

65 g grated sharp Cheddar cheese, divided

4 eggs

1 handful greens (rocket or spinach) per person,

rinsed and patted dry

Sea salt   Freshly ground black pepper

TOOLS / EQUIPMENT

Bread knife   Box grater

Toaster oven   Small cast-iron frying pan

Metal spatula

DIRECTIONS:

1. Drizzle a little olive oil onto the cut sides of the bread, and lay the slices on a toaster tray. Toast until golden and crispy, about 3 minutes. Turn the slices cut-side up, transfer to plates, and sprinkle the cheese evenly on the toast.

2. Return the bread to the toaster oven and broil until the cheese bubbles, about 5 minutes. Carefully transfer the toast to the plates.

3. In a small cast-iron frying pan over medium-high heat, fry the eggs in enough olive oil to coat the pan once it is hot. Turn the heat to medium after 1 minute, allowing the whites to cook fully while keeping the yolks soft. Season with salt and pepper.

4. Pile the greens onto the toast sandwich bottoms, followed by the fried egg; then top with grilled cheesy toast. Eat at once, with a plate underneath to catch any drips of liquidy golden yolk.

Chicken Skewer Sandwiches

Prep Time: 20 minutes, plus overnight to marinate,

Cook Time: 20 minutes, Serves:4

INGREDIENTS:

160 ml olive oil, plus extra for drizzling

80 ml red wine vinegar   2 lemons, juiced, and one zested

4 garlic cloves, chopped   1 tablespoon fresh thyme leaves

1 tablespoon fresh oregano leaves

1 tablespoon fresh basil leaves,

1 teaspoon red pepper flakes, or to taste   1 bay leaf

1 teaspoon sugar   1 teaspoon salt

1 teaspoon freshly ground black pepper

455 g boneless chicken thighs, cut into 4 cm cubes

1 baguette, cut into 4 sections, each split open lengthwise

1 tablespoon coarsely chopped fresh mint or parsley, or a mix, for garnish

TOOLS / EQUIPMENT

Citrus reamer   Zester

Bread knife   Large bowl

Metal skewers   Tongs

Grill pan

DIRECTIONS:

1. In a large bowl, stir together the olive oil, vinegar, lemon juice and zest, garlic, thyme, oregano, basil, red pepper flakes, bay leaf, sugar, salt, and pepper. Add the cubed chicken and refrigerate, covered tightly or in a large, resealable bag, overnight to marinate.

2. Thread the chicken onto skewers, folding the meat on itself to skewer if it is uneven. Heat a grill pan over high heat until hot. Grill the chicken for 3 to 5 minutes per side, until cooked through and charred in spots.

3. Transfer the grilled skewers to a large plate while you grill the bread. Drizzle olive oil onto the bread and grill for 3 to 5 minutes apiece, rotating as needed, until blackened in spots.

4. These skewers are delicious laid on top of the grilled bread with a scatter of chopped fresh herbs—like parsley or mint—to garnish.

Lemon-Blueberry Shortbread Tart

Prep Time: 10 minutes, Cook Time: 1 hour 5

minutes, plus 1 hour 15 minutes to rest a, Serves:6

INGREDIENTS:

FOR THE CRUST

Nonstick cooking spray

14 tablespoons cold butter, cut into 1 cm cubes

185 g plain flour   100 g sugar

FOR THE CUSTARD

370 g fresh blueberries   3 large eggs

175 g granulated sugar   Juice of 2 large lemons

30 g plan flour   30 g icing sugar

TOOLS/EQUIPMENT

Knife   8- or 23 cm springform pan

Rimmed baking sheet   Pastry cutter (optional)

2 medium bowls   Whisk

Toothpick (optional)   Mesh strainer (optional)

DIRECTIONS:

1. Preheat the oven to 200°C. Spray an 8- or 23 cm springform pan with cooking spray. Place the pan on a rimmed baking sheet.

2. In a medium bowl, combine the butter, flour, and sugar. Use a pastry cutter or clean fingers to cut in the butter until the mixture forms coarse crumbs. Press the crust mixture into the bottom of the prepared pan. Bake for 16 to 20 minutes, or just until the crust begins to turn lightly golden in colour. Remove from the oven and reduce the temperature to 160°C.

3. Reduce the oven temperature to 160°C.

4. Scatter the blueberries over the crust. In a medium bowl, whisk the eggs and granulated sugar until thick and frothy, about 2 minutes. Add the lemon juice and flour, and whisk until blended and smooth. Pour the custard mixture over the crust with the blueberries.

5. Bake until the custard is set, 35 to 45 minutes It is done if it jiggles only slightly when the pan is shaken a bit, and the center is not wet.

6. Allow the tart to rest for 15 minutes. Run a sharp knife gently around the crust, then slowly release the pan. After you see that the sides have released, close the pan back up and allow to cool for an hour at room temperature. Chill in the refrigerator until ready to serve.

7. Just before serving, use a mesh strainer to dust the tart with icing sugar.

German Chocolate Brownies

Prep Time: 25 minutes , Cook Time: 1 hour 10 minutes (plus cooling), Serves:36 brownies

INGREDIENTS:

BROWNIES

115 g butter   200 g sweet baking chocolate

200 g packed brown sugar   3 large eggs

1 teaspoon vanilla extract   125 g plain flour

½ teaspoon salt

GERMAN CHOCOLATE TOPPING

3 large egg whites   155 g sweetened flaked coconut

110 g pecans, toasted and chopped

100 g packed brown sugar   60 ml whole milk

½ teaspoon vanilla extract

⅛ teaspoon almond extract   ⅛ teaspoon salt

DIRECTIONS:

1. Preheat oven to 175°C. Grease a 13 x 23 cm metal baking pan.

2. Prepare Brownies: In 3-litre saucepan, melt butter and chocolate over medium-low heat, stirring frequently. Remove saucepan from heat; stir in sugar. Stir in eggs, 1 at a time, until well blended. Add vanilla. Stir in flour and salt just until blended. Spread batter in prepared baking pan.

3. Prepare German Chocolate Topping: In medium bowl with wire whisk, beat egg whites until foamy. Stir in coconut, pecans, sugar, milk, extracts, and salt until well combined. Spread topping evenly over brownies.

4. Bake for 45 to 50 minutes or until toothpick inserted in brownies 5 cm from edge comes out almost clean and topping turns golden brown. Cool brownies completely in pan on wire rack.

Mini Orange Cookie Tarts

Prep Time: 30 minutes (plus 30 minutes chill time), Cook Time: 25 minutes, Serves:20 tarts

INGREDIENTS:

FOR THE CRUST

115 g unsalted butter, at room temperature

60 g icing sugar   125 g plain flour

⅛ teaspoon table salt

FOR THE FILLING

120 ml plus 2 tablespoons sweetened condensed milk

60 ml freshly squeezed orange juice (1 or 2 oranges)

2 tablespoons orange zest   2 large egg yolks

½ teaspoon orange extract

¼ teaspoon vanilla extract

TOOLS/EQUIPMENT:

2 medium bowls   Electric hand mixer

Whisk or fork   Zester

Mini muffin pan

DIRECTIONS:

1. Preheat the oven to 160˚C.

2. In a medium bowl, beat the butter with an electric mixer on medium speed for about 10 seconds, or until smooth. Add the sugar, beating until well blended and light and fluffy, about 2 minutes. Beat in the flour and salt until just combined.

3. In another medium bowl, whisk together the milk, orange juice, zest, yolks, orange extract, and vanilla until well blended.

4. Press a rounded teaspoon of cookie dough in about 20 cups of an ungreased 24-cup mini muffin pan. Press in the center to push the dough up the sides of each pan cup to form a little cookie cup. Spoon about 2 teaspoons of the filling into each cookie cup, or until each cup is about ¾ full.

5. Bake for 20 to 25 minutes, or until filling is set and cookies are golden brown. Cool slightly in pan, then finish cooling in refrigerator for about 30 minutes, or until chilled.

Strawberry-Rhubarb Mini Tarts

Prep Time: 30 minutes plus 1 hour to chill, Cook Time: 45 minutes, Serves:8

INGREDIENTS:

FOR THE DOUGH

310 g plain flour

1 teaspoon sugar, plus 1 teaspoon for sprinkling

1 teaspoon salt

460 g butter, freezer-cold and chopped into small cubes

60 ml ice water

FOR THE FILLING

340 g rhubarb, rinsed, ends trimmed, cut into ½ cm pieces

600 g fresh strawberries, rinsed and hulled, cut into ½ cm pieces

100 g sugar	Zest of 1 orange
60 ml orange juice	Pinch salt

TOOLS/ EQUIPMENT

Zester	Food processor
Plastic wrap	Large bowl
Rolling pin	2 baking sheets
Parchment paper	Pastry brush
Wire cooling rack	

DIRECTIONS:

1. In a food processor, pulse the flour, sugar, and salt to combine. Add the cold butter and pulse 5 to 7 times, until the butter mixes with the flour to form pea-size crumbs. In a slow stream, add the ice water while pulsing, stopping once the dough holds together.

2. To test, unplug the food processor, open the lid, and press some dough together. If it holds together, it's ready. If it still crumbles, add a bit more ice water as you pulse a few more times. You may use slightly less or slightly more than 60 ml of water.

3. Separate the dough into two mounds, then flatten each to form a disk. Cut the plastic wrap in two between the disks, and wrap each. Refrigerate for at least 20 minutes to let it firm up.

4. In a large bowl, carefully mix together the rhubarb, strawberries, sugar, orange zest, orange juice, and salt. Cover with plastic wrap, and let the flavours meld, at least 15 minutes.

5. On a lightly floured surface, cut each disk into four. Chill the rest as you roll each one out. Roll from the center to the edge, turning an eighth turn with each pass of the rolling pin, until the dough is ½ cm thick. (They don't have to be perfect circles. Patch any large tears with dough pinched from the edge.)

6. Line two baking sheets with parchment paper, and lay the rolled pastry 5 – 8 cm apart from each another. Spoon mounds of the fruit mixture into the center of each pastry, dividing the filling evenly and leaving a 2.5 cm border around the edge. Assemble one set of tarts at a time, leaving the other batch of pastry in the refrigerator.

7. Gather the pastry edges, making pleats onto the piled fruit. Lightly brush water in between the folds to press the pastry together and keep it in place. If the dough becomes flabby, it needs to be rechilled.

8. Once you have filled and crimped all the tarts, refrigerate them for at least 1 hour before baking.

9. Repeat through 8 with the remaining dough.

10. Preheat the oven to 200°C.

11. Very lightly brush the edges of the pastry with water, and sprinkle with the reserved 1 teaspoon of sugar. Bake for 30 minutes, or until the crusts are golden, then lower the temperature to 190°C and bake for 10 to 15 minutes, until the juices bubble and the crust is deeply golden. Transfer the tarts to a wire cooling rack to cool.

12. Remove the tarts when they can be easily handled, and enjoy them warm. Store leftover tarts at room temperature, wrapped loosely in foil, for 2 days.

Rocky Road Brownies

Prep Time: 25 minutes, Cook Time: 50 minutes (plus cooling), Serves:24 brownies

INGREDIENTS:

155 g plain flour	½ teaspoon baking powder	2 teaspoons vanilla extract	5 large eggs
½ teaspoon salt	180 g butter	100 g miniature marshmallows	
150 g unsweetened chocolate	400 g sugar	195 g assorted nuts, toasted and coarsely chopped	

DIRECTIONS:

1. Preheat oven to 175°C. Grease a 13 x 23 cm metal baking pan.

2. In medium bowl with wire whisk, mix flour, baking powder, and salt. In 3-litre saucepan, melt butter and chocolate over medium-low heat, stirring frequently. Remove saucepan from heat; stir in sugar and vanilla. Stir in eggs, 1 at a time, until well blended. Stir in flour mixture just until blended. Spread batter in prepared baking pan.

3. Bake for 20 minutes or until toothpick inserted in brownies 5 cm from edge comes out almost clean. Sprinkle brownies evenly with marshmallows; top with nuts. Bake for 5 minutes longer or until marshmallows melt slightly. Cool brownies completely in pan on wire rack.

4. When cool, cut brownies lengthwise into 4 strips, then cut each strip crosswise into 6 pieces.

Chocolate-Pomegranate Brownies

Prep Time: 10 minutes, Cook Time: 30 minutes, Serves:12

INGREDIENTS:

300 g semisweet dark chocolate, chopped, divided	
445 g butter, cut into cubes	4 eggs
250 g light brown sugar	125 g plain flour
Seeds from ½ fresh pomegranate, for topping	

TOOLS / EQUIPMENT

Double boiler	Rubber spatula
Parchment paper	Baking dish
Large bowl	Electric mixer
Skewer or toothpick	Wire cooling rack

DIRECTIONS:

1. Preheat the oven to 175°C.

2. Using a double boiler, melt half the chocolate and all the butter. Be careful that the water doesn't bubble up into the top saucepan as you do so, or it will ruin the chocolate. Remove the melted chocolate pan from the hot water bath, wipe the base with a dry dish towel to ensure no drips, stir the butter-chocolate mixture together, and set aside.

3. Line a square or small rectangular baking dish with parchment long enough that the paper extends beyond edges by at least 5 cm on all sides.

4. In a large bowl, use a fork or hand mixer to thoroughly combine the eggs, sugar, and flour. Add the slightly cooled, melted chocolate mixture and the remaining portion of chopped chocolate, stirring to combine.

5. Pour the mixture into the prepared baking dish, and bake for 25 minutes, or until a skewer or toothpick comes out almost clean. If you jiggle the tin, the center should move just a little.

6. Cool the brownies on a wire cooling rack for 10 minutes in the pan; then, using the parchment tabs on either side, lift the brownies out.

7. Cut the brownies into squares, and scatter the pomegranate seeds on top. Enjoy the delicious combo of still-molten chocolate and tart, juicy pomegranate!

Chapter 9: Pies

Tender Banana Cream Pie

Prep Time: 30 minutes (plus 5 hours chill time), Cook Time: 45 minutes, Serves:1 pie (serves 8)

INGREDIENTS:

FOR THE PIE

Flour, for dusting the work surface

1 chilled pie case

2 large egg yolks   175 g granulated sugar

30 g cornflour   ¼ teaspoon table salt

720 ml milk   3 tablespoons unsalted butter

1 teaspoon vanilla extract

2 large firm, ripe bananas, thinly sliced

FOR THE WHIPPED CREAM

360 g cold heavy whipping cream

2 tablespoons granulated sugar

TOOLS/EQUIPMENT:

Rolling pin   23 cm pie pan

Parchment paper or aluminum foil

Pie weights or dried beans (optional)

Small bowl   Large saucepan

Whisk or spoon   Large bowl

DIRECTIONS:

1. Roll out the prepared chilled pie dough on a lightly floured surface to about ½ cm thick. Transfer the dough into a 23 cm pie pan. Trim the extra dough around the edges, and crimp or flute the edges as desired. Refrigerate for at least 20 to 30 minutes, or until cold.

2. Preheat the oven to 190˚C.

3. Line the crust with parchment paper or aluminum foil. Top with pie weights or dried beans, if desired. Lightly cover the outer rim of the crust with foil to prevent over-browning. Bake for 15 to 20 minutes, or until very light golden brown. Remove the pie weights or beans and paper and foil from the crust. Lightly poke any air bubbles that may have formed in the crust to flatten the dough. Set aside to cool.

4. In a small bowl, beat the egg yolks, then set aside. In a large saucepan over medium-high heat, whisk together 150 g of sugar, the cornflour, salt, and milk. Whisking frequently, cook until very thick, 10 to 20 minutes. While whisking, spoon a little of the hot milk mixture into the bowl with the eggs. Slowly spoon in more milk until the eggs are warm. Pour the remaining milk mixture and the egg mixture into the saucepan. Bring the mixture to a gentle boil and cook 2 to 3 minutes longer, whisking constantly. Remove the pan from heat, and stir in the butter and vanilla until the butter has melted.

5. Pour the filling into a large bowl, cover with plastic wrap, and refrigerate for at least 30 minutes, or until cold.

6. Arrange the banana slices evenly over the bottom of the pan. Pour the custard filling over the bananas.

7. In a large cold bowl, whip the heavy cream and 2 tablespoons of sugar with an electric mixer on medium-high speed until soft peaks form.

8. Spread the whipped cream on top of the pie. Refrigerate for 4 to 6 hours or overnight. Serve cold.

Black-Bottom Chocolate Cream Pie

Prep Time: 45 MINUTES, Cook Time: 55 minutes (plus cooling and chilling), Serves:12

INGREDIENTS:

24 wafer biscuits, pulsed in food processor with knife blade attached

6 tablespoons butter

200 g plus 3 tablespoons sugar

40 g cornflour

¼ teaspoon salt

840 ml whole milk

4 large egg yolks

75 g unsweetened chocolate, finely chopped

240 g heavy cream   semisweet chocolate curls, for garnish

DIRECTIONS:

1. Preheat oven to 190°C. In the microwave, melt 4 tablespoons butter in, microwave-safe bowl; add wafer crumbs and 1 tablespoon sugar. Stir until moistened. Firmly press mixture into bottom and up side of 23 cm pie plate. Bake for 10 to 12 minutes or until set. Cool crust completely on wire rack.
2. In heavy 3-litre saucepan with wire whisk, mix cornflour, salt, and 200 g sugar. While whisking, gradually add milk until blended. Cook over medium-high heat for 7 to 8 minutes or until boiling and thickened, whisking constantly. Remove saucepan from heat.
3. In large bowl with wire whisk, beat egg yolks until blended. Whisk in hot milk mixture in steady stream. Return mixture to saucepan and cook over medium heat for 4 to 6 minutes or until mixture boils and thickens, stirring constantly. Remove saucepan from heat and add chocolate. Stir until melted, then stir in remaining 2 tablespoons butter until melted.
4. Pour filling into cooled piecrust and spread evenly. Press sheet of plastic wrap directly against surface. Refrigerate at least 4 hours or up to overnight, or until cold and stiff.
5. In large bowl with mixer on medium-high speed, beat cream until thickened. While beating, gradually add remaining 2 tablespoons sugar. Beat until soft peaks form. Dollop over pie. Garnish with chocolate curls, if using.

Caramel Apple Streusel Pie

Prep Time: 30 minutes, Cook Time: 60 minutes, Serves:1 pie (serves 8)

INGREDIENTS:

FOR THE STREUSEL CRUMB TOPPING

65 g plain flour   50 g brown sugar

½ teaspoon cinnamon   ⅛ teaspoon table salt

4 tablespoons cold unsalted butter, cubed

FOR THE PIE

160 g thick caramel ice cream topping

3 tablespoons plain flour   ¼ teaspoon cinnamon

¼ teaspoon table salt

1.1 kg, peeled, thinly sliced cooking apples such as Granny Smith

1 chilled ready-made pie case

Flour, for dusting the work surface

TOOLS/EQUIPMENT:

Small bowl   Pastry cutter

Large bowl   Rolling pin

23 cm pie pan   Aluminum foil

Baking sheet

DIRECTIONS:

1. Preheat the oven to 190°C.
2. In a small bowl, mix together 65 g of flour, brown sugar, ½ teaspoon of cinnamon, and ⅛ teaspoon of salt until well blended. With a pastry cutter or the back of a fork, cut in the cold butter cubes until it forms coarse crumbs.
3. In a large bowl, whisk together the caramel topping, 3 tablespoons of flour, ¼ teaspoon of cinnamon, and ¼ teaspoon of salt until well blended. Gently stir in the apples until blended.
4. Roll out the chilled pie case on a lightly floured surface to about ½ cm thick. Transfer to a 23 cm pie pan. Cut off the excess dough around the edges of the pan.
5. Spoon the apples into the pie crust. Sprinkle streusel over the top. Flute or crimp the pie crust as desired. Cover the edges of the pie crust with aluminum foil.
6. Place the pie on a baking sheet. Bake for about 40 minutes. Remove the foil from edges, then bake for an additional 20 minutes, or until the apples are soft. Cool before slicing and serving.

Creamy Mango Pie

Prep Time: 10 minutes, Cook Time: 1 hour and 20 minutes plus cooling and chilling, Serves:1

INGREDIENTS:

For the crust:

10 digestive biscuits

115 g unsalted butter, melted

1 ½ tablespoons granulated white sugar

For the mango filling:

330 g frozen and thawed mango chunks

1 (350 g) can condensed milk

50 g granulated white sugar   3 large eggs

Zest of 1 lemon   Juice of 1 lemon

½ teaspoon vanilla extract   ⅛ teaspoon salt

Whipped cream or mango slices, for serving

TOOLS/EQUIPMENT

Zip-top bag   Rolling pin

Measuring cups and spoons   Mixing bowl

Wooden spoon   23 cmdeep-dish pie pan

Oven-safe gloves   Blender or food processor

Zester

DIRECTIONS:

To make the crust:

1. Preheat your oven to 175°C.
2. Put the digestive biscuits in a zip-top bag, and seal it. Using a rolling pin, smash the biscuits They do not have to be super fine crumbs.
3. In a mixing bowl, stir together the biscuit crumbs, melted butter, and granulated white sugar. Use the back of a measuring cup to press the crust down into a 23 cm deep dish pie pan.
4. Put the pie pan in the oven. Bake for 10 minutes, or until the crust is lightly browned on the edges.

To make the filling:

1. While the piecrust is baking, put the mango in a blender or food processor. Blend until totally smooth.
2. Add the condensed milk, granulated white sugar, eggs, lemon zest and juice, vanilla, and salt. Blend until fully combined.
3. Using oven-safe gloves, remove the pie pan from the oven. Pour the filling into the piecrust. Return the pie pan to the oven. Bake for 40 minutes, or until the filling is slightly set on the edges while still slightly jiggly in the center.
4. Using oven-safe gloves, remove the pie pan from the oven. Let the pie cool for 1 hour. Refrigerate for at least 2 hours, or until set.
5. Top the pie with whipped cream or mango slices.

Little Chicken And Mushroom Biscuit Pot Pies

Prep Time: 40 minutes, Cook Time: 20 minutes, Serves:serves 4

INGREDIENTS:

FOR THE FILLING

4 tablespoons unsalted butter

100 g thinly sliced and coarsely chopped mushrooms

40 g finely chopped onion

35 g finely chopped celery

30 g finely chopped carrot   1 garlic clove, minced

30 g plain flour   300 ml chicken stock

120 g heavy whipping cream

⅛ teaspoon table salt

⅛ teaspoon freshly ground black pepper

140 g shredded precooked chicken

FOR THE BISCUIT TOPPING

125 g plain flour   1 teaspoon baking powder

¼ teaspoon table salt

4 tablespoons cold unsalted butter, cut into small cubes

80 ml cold milk

TOOLS/EQUIPMENT:

4 (200 g) ramekins   Baking sheet

Large frying pan   Medium bowl

Pastry cutter (see Cutting in Butter)

DIRECTIONS:

1. In a large frying pan over medium heat, melt 4 tablespoons of butter. Add the mushrooms, onion, celery, carrot, and garlic. Cook 4 to 5 minutes, or until soft, stirring occasionally.
2. Stir in 30 g of flour to the frying pan. Once incorporated, slowly stir in the broth and cream until smooth. Cook and stir until thickened and bubbly, 2 to 3 minutes. Stir in ⅛ teaspoon of salt, the black pepper, and shredded chicken. Spoon the mixture into the ramekins.
3. In a medium bowl, mix together 125 g of flour, baking powder, and ¼ teaspoon of salt until well blended. Cut in 4 tablespoons of cold butter with a pastry cutter or the back of a fork until the mixture is crumbly. Mix in the milk, stirring until the dough is just combined. Spoon the biscuit dough in small pieces over the filling in the ramekins.
4. Bake for 15 to 20 minutes, or until the biscuit topping is golden brown. Cool slightly before serving.

Double-Crust Blueberry Pie

Prep Time: 20 minutes, Cook Time: 60 minutes, Serves:1 pie (serves 8)

INGREDIENTS:

590 g fresh blueberries

100 g granulated sugar, plus 1 tablespoon for the topping

65 g plain flour

1 teaspoon freshly grated lemon zest

2 tablespoons freshly squeezed lemon juice (about 1 lemon)

Flour, for dusting the work surface

2 chilled pie cases   1 egg, lightly beaten

TOOLS/EQUIPMENT:

Large bowl	Zester
23 cm pie pan	Rolling pin
Pastry brush	Baking sheet

DIRECTIONS:

1. Preheat the oven to 205˚C.

2. In a large bowl, gently stir together the blueberries, 100 g of sugar, the flour, lemon zest, and lemon juice until blended.

3. Roll out each prepared chilled pie dough crust on a lightly floured surface to about ½ cm thick. Gently transfer one to a 23 cm pie pan. Cut off any excess dough around edges.

4. Spoon the blueberry mixture over the dough in the pie pan. Gently place the second dough on top. Press the edges together with a fork or crimp or flute as desired to form a nice seal. With a pastry brush, brush a little beaten egg over the crust, then cut 3 to 5 slits in the top pie crust with a sharp knife. Sprinkle 1 tablespoon of sugar on top.

5. Place the pie on a baking sheet. Bake for 45 to 60 minutes, or until the pie is golden brown and the filling is bubbly. Cool completely before slicing and serving.

Peachy Pecan Crumb Pie

Prep Time: 35 minutes, Cook Time: 1 hour 35 minutes (plus chilling and cooling), Serves:8

INGREDIENTS:

CRUMB TOPPING

65 g plain flour   20 g oats, uncooked

50 g packed brown sugar   30 g chopped pecans

½ teaspoon freshly grated lemon peel

⅛ teaspoon salt

3 tablespoons butter, softened

FILLING

900 g ripe peaches (about 7 to 8 large), peeled and chopped

100 g packed brown sugar   2 tablespoons cornflour

¼ teaspoon ground cinnamon

1 tablespoon lemon juice

vanilla ice cream, for serving

DIRECTIONS:

1. Prepare Pie Shell: On lightly floured surface with lightly floured rolling pin, roll dough out into 33 cm circle. Transfer to 23 cm pie plate. Gently press dough against bottom and up side of plate without stretching it. If necessary, trim dough so overhang is even (about 1 cm from edge of rim). Fold overhang under itself and crimp as desired. Refrigerate pie shell for 30 minutes.

2. Prepare Crumb Topping: Meanwhile, place foil-lined, rimmed baking sheet in oven and preheat to 220°C. In medium bowl, with your hands, combine flour, oats, brown sugar, pecans, lemon peel, and salt. Add butter and squeeze to form small clumps. Refrigerate until ready to use.

Old-Fashioned Strawberry Pie

Prep Time: 45 minutes (plus 2 hours and 20 minutes chill time, Cook Time: 20 minutes, Serves:1 pie (serves 8)

INGREDIENTS:

Flour, for dusting the work surface

1 chilled pie case

1 kg fresh strawberries, stems removed and sliced, divided

160 ml – 240 ml water   175 g granulated sugar

3 tablespoons cornflour

TOOLS/EQUIPMENT:

Rolling pin   23 cm pie pan

Parchment paper and/or aluminum foil

Pie weights or dried beans (optional)   Blender

Large saucepan   Whisk or fork

DIRECTIONS:

1. Roll out the chilled pie dough on a lightly floured surface to about ½ cm thick. Transfer the dough to a 23 cm pie pan. Trim the extra dough around the edges, and crimp or flute the edges as desired. Refrigerate for at least 20 to 30 minutes, or until cold.

2. Preheat the oven to 190˚C.

3. Line the crust with parchment paper or aluminum foil. Top with pie weights or dried beans, if using. Lightly cover the outer rim of the crust with aluminum foil to prevent over-browning. Bake for 15 to 20 minutes, or until very light golden brown. Remove the pie weights or beans and paper or foil from the crust. Lightly poke any air bubbles that may have formed around the crust to flatten the dough. Set aside to cool.

4. Place 150 g of strawberries and 160 ml of water in a blender, and process until smooth. Add more water as needed so you have 1½ cups of berry mixture.

5. In a large saucepan, whisk together the sugar and cornflour. Whisk in the blended berry mixture. Place the saucepan over medium-high heat. Cook for 5 to 7 minutes, stirring, until bubbly and thickened. Remove from the heat to cool.

6. Spread about ¼ cup of glaze over the bottom and sides of the pie crust. Add the remaining whole strawberries into the pan with the glaze, stir to mix, then spoon the blended strawberries over the glaze in the pie crust into an even layer. Place the pie in the refrigerator

Southern Chocolate Walnut Pie

Prep Time: 30 minutes (20 minutes chill time, plus cooling time), Cook Time: 65 minutes, Serves:1 pie (serves 8)

INGREDIENTS:

Flour, for dusting the work surface

1 chilled pie case

175 g granulated sugar   65 g plain flour

50 g brown sugar   ¼ teaspoon table salt

2 large eggs, at room temperature

115 g unsalted butter, melted and cooled

1 teaspoon vanilla extract   145 g chopped walnuts

170 g semisweet chocolate chips

TOOLS/EQUIPMENT:

Rolling pin   23 cm pie pan

Parchment paper and/or aluminum foil

Pie weights or dried beans (optional)

Large bowl   Whisk or fork

Baking sheet

DIRECTIONS:

1. Roll out the chilled pie dough on a lightly floured surface to about ½ cm thick. Transfer the dough to a 23 cm pie pan. Trim the extra dough around the edges, and crimp or flute the edges as desired (see Pie Fluting: How To). Return to the refrigerator for at least 20 to 30 minutes, or until cold.

2. Preheat the oven to 190˚C.

3. Line the crust with parchment paper or aluminum foil. Top with pie weights or dried beans, if using. Lightly cover the outer rim of the crust with aluminum foil to prevent over-browning. Bake for 15 to 20 minutes, or until very light golden brown. Leave the foil in place around the edge of the pie crust, but remove the weights or beans and paper or foil from the bottom of the crust. Lightly poke any air bubbles that may have formed around crust to flatten the dough.

4. Lower the oven temperature to 160˚C.

5. In a large bowl, whisk together the granulated sugar, flour, brown sugar, and salt until well blended. Whisk in the eggs, melted butter, and vanilla until blended. Stir in the walnuts and chocolate chips.

6. Place the pie pan on a baking sheet, then pour the filling over the crust, spreading the walnuts and chocolate chips to evenly distribute. Bake for about 25 minutes, remove the foil from the crust, then bake an additional 10 to 20 minutes, or until the filling appears set (firm). Cool completely before slicing.

Mini Pot Pies

Prep Time: 15 minutes, Cook Time: 1 hour, Serves:4

INGREDIENTS:

1 sheet frozen puff pastry, thawed in refrigerator

2 tablespoons plain flour, plus more for dusting surface

4 tablespoons unsalted butter

1 shallot, finely chopped

2 teaspoons fresh thyme leaves

240 ml chicken stock

240 ml whole milk   Salt

Freshly ground black pepper   4 carrots, peeled and sliced

420 g shredded or diced leftover chicken or turkey

190 g frozen peas, thawed

90 g white pearl onions, peeled

5 g chopped fresh flat-leaf parsley

 Hot sauce, to taste

1 egg, lightly beaten

TOOLS / EQUIPMENT

Vegetable peeler	Rolling pin
Parchment paper	Baking sheet
Large cast-iron frying pan	Whisk
Ladle	4 ramekins
Pastry brush	

DIRECTIONS:

1. Preheat the oven to 200°C.
2. Unfold the pastry, and gently roll it out on a lightly floured work surface to ½ cm thick. Cut it into 4 equal-size pieces slightly larger than the size of your ramekins. Lay them out onto parchment paper, transfer to a baking sheet, and refrigerate until ready to use.
3. In a large cast-iron frying pan over medium heat, heat the butter. When it is melted and bubbling, add the shallot and thyme, and cook until the shallot becomes translucent, about 4 minutes, stirring regularly. Add the flour and cook, whisking constantly, until the mixture is golden and fully incorporated, about 5 minutes.
4. Whisk in the stock gradually, incorporating the first half completely before adding the remainder. Whisk in the milk, and season with salt and pepper. Bring to a boil, then reduce heat and simmer, whisking occasionally, until the mixture is thick enough to coat a spoon, 10 to 12 minutes. Add the carrots and cook until just tender, 3 to 5 minutes. Add the chicken, peas, onions, and parsley; season with hot sauce, salt, and pepper; and stir to combine.
5. Ladle the mixture into 4 ramekins or mini casseroles assembled on a baking sheet. Drape puff pastry over filling, ensuring that it hangs over ramekin edges. Gently press on the edges to seal. Brush the pastry with the beaten egg, and make a slit in the centers with a sharp knife for steam to escape while baking.
6. Bake until the puff pastry surfaces are golden and the filling is bubbling through the slits, 15 to 20 minutes. Reduce the heat to 175°C, and bake until the puff pastry is deeply golden and cooked through, 10 to 15 minutes longer.
7. Let sit for 10 minutes before serving on large plates.

Conclusion

So, kids, are you ready to do some cooking by yourself? Well, then put on your apron and your chef hats to get started. Remember, focus on one recipe at a time and start with something simple and basic. Learn a little cooking every day; soon, you will become a great chef. Happy Cooking!